Get Fit With Your Dog

Get Fit With Your Dog

A COMPANION GUIDE TO HEALTH

KAREN SULLIVAN

All inquiries should be addressed to:
Barron's Educational Series, Inc.
250 Wireless Blvd.
Hauppauge, NY 11788
www.barronseduc.com

ISBN-13: 978-0-7641-3905-5
ISBN-10: 0-7641-3905-3

Library of Congress Catalog No.: 2007935673

Printed and bound in Thailand

9 8 7 6 5 4 3 2 1

This book was conceived, designed, and produced by **Ivy Press**

Creative Director Peter Bridgewater
Publisher Jason Hook
Editorial Director Caroline Earle
Art Director Sarah Howerd
Senior Project Editor Mary Todd
Designer Ginny Zeal
Photographer Nick Ridley
Illustrators Joanna Kerr, John Woodcock
Picture Researcher Emma Brown

Contents

Foreword

As a dog (and cat) loving person who enjoys being active outdoors, I am very interested in the topic of this book. Dogs have been a part of my life for most of my life. The dogs in my life have always been a welcome excuse to get out and go for a hike and visit places that I may not have explored on my own. At other times, when it was the last thing I wanted to do, my dogs were the sole motivation to get me outside and active.

As a veterinarian, the concept of human and canine companion fitness is of great interest to me. Veterinarians are trained to recognize optimal weight and body condition of pets, and it is our duty to inform owners if we find their pet to be overweight or underweight. Most often, as you can probably guess, it is a case of the pet being overweight. I have often found myself explaining this to the owners, who were either surprised to hear their pets were overweight, didn't believe they were overweight, or seemed not to care that they were overweight. In addition, for many of those consultations, I found that the pets' humans were also overweight. This made for an awkward situation, because I felt the issues were deeper than simply cutting back on the pets' snacks or changing their diet.

This book is a great start for people to learn about and assess their body type, weight, eating habits, and fitness levels as objectively as possible, and include their canine companions at the same time. Helpful assessment tools, nutrition tips, and exercise ideas for humans are interwoven with solid tips and advice for their dogs. If achieving an optimal weight, feeling more energetic and alert, and experiencing a myriad of physiological benefits doesn't provide sufficient motivation to start a fitness program, maybe the extra boost of knowing that your pet is benefiting in a similar way will.

I admit to sometimes taking shortcuts and seeking out the more level path while walking my dogs. I appreciated the commonsense tips in this book such as varying the terrain, and wearing a pedometer to increase both fitness levels and awareness of exercise on a daily basis; by simply altering my walk I can easily increase the workout level.

Getting fit is not an overnight process for humans or for dogs. Rather, it is a combination of exercise, nutrition, and lifestyle changes together with a change in some habits. This book offers a great way to assess fitness levels and to begin and develop a fitness plan for a healthier way of life for dogs and their humans. Dogs have been called "man's best friend"—now it is our turn to be their best friends.

Janet Tobiassen DVM

About.com Guide
www.about.com

Left A lively dog is the perfect motivation to get out and explore places that you might not go to on your own.

Introduction

Below A few simple changes to the food your dog eats can have a dramatic impact on his health and well-being.

Expanding waistlines and related health problems have been a cause for international concern for several years. In the US, more than 70 percent of adults and at least 30 percent of children are now overweight or obese, and it's a problem that has officially reached epidemic proportions. It's a trend that shows no sign of slowing, despite widespread media interest, government initiatives, and educational efforts by the fitness and food industries, doctors and medical associations, and consumer groups.

And it's not just people who are getting fatter and suffering from debilitating health problems; our pet population is suffering the same fate. Recent statistics show that more than 40 percent of all dogs (and cats) are now overweight or obese. Veterinary Pet Insurance (VPI), the nation's oldest and largest provider of pet health insurance, found that it reimbursed more than $14 million last year for claims with links to pet obesity. Claims related to obesity accounted for 7 percent of all medical claims submitted to VPI in 2006.

The simple truth is that animal-loving couch potatoes are passing on their unhealthy habits to their pets—adopting a lifestyle that threatens their health and could end up shortening their lives. When was the last time you and your dog were breathless after a session in the local park? Can either of you say no to tempting snacks and treats? Has your dog's girth expanded at the same rate as your own? Are you both suffering from nagging health problems that prevent you from embracing life with energy and enthusiasm? If you answered yes to any one of these questions, this book is for you.

A few simple changes to the way you live your life—the food you eat and the exercise you do on a daily basis—can have a dramatic impact on your health and well-being, and both you and your dog will not only lose weight and become fit in the process, but will also experience a stronger bond and increase your chances of a longer life.

Having a dog can be rewarding and great fun. The lessons, tips, and ideas you will find throughout this book will provide you with all you need to get fit and shed those unwanted pounds and inches safely, gradually, and effectively—with minimal effort and plenty of variety and enjoyment. So put your feet up (for the last time) and read on to find out the best ways to improve your health on many levels, in the company of your canine companion. Then watch the changes begin to happen. Love me, love my dog? Now's the time to show your dog how much you really care about the future you can, and will, have together.

Left Playing and exercising daily with your dog will help strengthen the bond between you.

Before you begin

Studies show that most adults are unaware of exactly how much they weigh (often underestimating by more than 25 percent of their body weight) and believe they are "fit enough," despite evidence to the contrary. What's more, the vast majority of dog owners don't really know if their pets are overweight until they visit their veterinarian for another reason. Our collective ability to self-delude can have serious long-term health problems, and it's time we faced up to them.

First and foremost, are you and your dog overweight? Are your fitness levels optimal for your age and build? How will those extra pounds and inches affect your lives—both now and in the future? Is your head stuck firmly in the sand?

It's time to sit up and take note. In this section we'll look at some ways to assess whether you and your dog are living a healthy lifestyle, and whether those love handles, potbellies, and flabby abs spell out danger in the years ahead. We've got comprehensive questionnaires to figure out where your lifestyle (and your dog's) is falling short, and some easy ways to establish whether you and your dog really are overweight—and by how much. More important, perhaps, we'll look at the real reasons why you and your dog need to get fit—not just to lose those unwanted pounds, but to live life to the fullest.

Why get fit?

Fitness is not about being thin, or having a small waist or bulging muscles. It is a combination of factors that enables us to function at our full potential when we engage in physical activity, and helps us to lose weight or maintain a healthy weight.

Above An enthusiastic pet can help you reach your goals far faster than exercising on your own.

Physical fitness involves the entire body: your heart, lungs, muscles, endurance, and mental capacity. People who are physically fit have greater stamina, strength, and flexibility than those who are not. Moreover, fitness elevates mood and maintains cognitive functions such as memory and the ability to concentrate. Being unfit does not necessarily mean being unhealthy, but it does put people at greater risk for many diseases, including heart disease and diabetes, and makes it more difficult to perform everyday tasks with ease.

Watch your weight

One of the most dangerous effects of poor physical fitness is the risk of becoming overweight or obese, which compromises health on all levels and costs lives. Although being overweight is itself considered to be a disease by the World Health Organization, it also contributes to many other diseases, many of them debilitating and some of them life-threatening (*see opposite*).

Dogs are no strangers to the obesity epidemic either. Like their owners, they tend to overeat, snack too much, eat the wrong foods, underexercise, and choose passive relaxation over activity. And, like humans, they can also become accustomed to a lazy lifestyle and an unhealthy diet, both of which add up to trouble. On the flip side, exercise has a host of important benefits, which we will look at next.

A 2003 study found that the more overweight a person is, the greater the risk of developing many types of cancer.

The dangers of obesity

Being overweight or obese has a range of negative effects on the health and well-being of both you and your dog. Among them are an increased risk of developing the following:

For your dog
- Cancer
- Diabetes mellitus
- Damage to joints, bones, and ligaments
- Heart disease and increased blood pressure
- Difficulty in breathing
- Heat intolerance
- Decreased liver function
- Increased surgical and anesthetic risk
- Reproductive problems
- Digestive disorders
- Decreased immune function (in particular, canine distemper and salmonella)
- Skin and coat problems
- Decreased stamina
- Decreased quality and length of life

For you
- Cancer
- Type 2 diabetes
- Bone and joint problems, including osteoporosis, osteoarthritis, and gout
- Heart problems, including heart attack and congestive heart failure
- Breathing problems, sleep apnea (when you stop breathing briefly during sleep)
- High blood pressure
- Stroke
- Abnormal blood fats (which cause veins and arteries to become blocked)
- Kidney disease
- Gallstones and gallbladder disease
- Urinary incontinence
- Low energy and stamina
- Low self-esteem

The benefits of exercise

Not only does exercise help to keep weight in check, which prevents overweight, obesity, and its incumbent problems, but it also has a whole host of other benefits, many of which may surprise you!

Exercise strengthens the cardiovascular system and reduces the risk of heart disease and stroke. According to the American Heart Foundation, sedentary adults have a 30–40 percent higher risk of death from coronary heart disease than those who exercise three to four times a week.

Other physical benefits

Exercise dilates the blood vessels so that the heart can pump more efficiently to supply blood to the rest of the body. The result is

that blood pressure declines. It also inhibits artery-clogging deposits known as plaque by increasing the concentration of HDL (commonly known as "good cholesterol" because it clears excess cholesterol from the bloodstream) and decreasing the concentration of LDL (bad cholesterol) in the blood.

Regular exercise improves lung capacity and efficiency, which in turn increases oxygen concentration in the blood. The result is a higher level of energy, which may be low in people who are overweight.

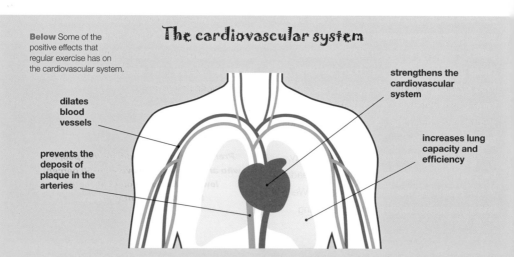

Below Some of the positive effects that regular exercise has on the cardiovascular system.

The cardiovascular system

dilates blood vessels

prevents the deposit of plaque in the arteries

strengthens the cardiovascular system

increases lung capacity and efficiency

stairs, and other activities that require your muscles to work against gravity) help preserve bone mass and may even increase it.

Psychological benefits

Regular exercise has a positive effect on mood, enhancing self-esteem and, for many people, relieving depression. Here's how:

● Exercise reduces stress, probably by calling on adrenaline to increase the flow of oxygen-rich blood to the muscles.
● Exercise stimulates secretion of endorphins, the feel-good hormones that are thought to elevate mood, heighten motivation, and increase tolerance of pain.
● Aerobic exercise helps improve and maintain concentration and alertness by increasing the supply of oxygen-rich blood to the brain.
● Regular exercise can also promote good, regular sleeping habits.

Your weight and bones

Exercise helps keep weight in check and allows you to increase your intake of calories without gaining weight. The reason is that exercise raises the rate at which your body converts food to energy, an important part of the process known as metabolism. Not only that, but several studies have found that regular exercise tends to reduce appetite.

As we grow older, our bones lose density, becoming thinner and more brittle. This leads to the debilitating disease osteoporosis. Weight-bearing exercises (such as hiking, climbing

Preliminary studies indicate that people who are more active have a 30–50 percent lower risk of developing diabetes than their sedentary peers.

The benefits for your dog

Dogs and humans aren't so very different when it comes to healthy living. Just like their owners, dogs will achieve a whole host of health benefits when they exercise regularly.

Right Dogs are naturally inclined to exercise, so give them free rein with plenty of games and fun.

Dogs gain the same benefits from exercise as do humans—and the evidence in favor is highly convincing. Exercise your dog to help keep his weight down; ward off disease; tone muscles; encourage healthy bones, joints, and ligaments; prevent certain types of cancer; reduce the risk of diabetes; promote healthy rest; and boost energy. And there's more:

Physical benefits

● Exercise helps to combat the negative effects of aging, such as arthritis and other problems associated with the joints, muscles, and bones.

● Exercise is an easy way to control weight. Adding one extra twenty-minute walk a day can significantly increase your dog's ability to burn calories and assist in weight loss.

● Increasing muscle mass through exercise can also raise your dog's metabolic rate so that he continues to burn off more calories all the time, even while resting.

● Exercise reduces the incidence of digestive problems and constipation.

Psychological benefits

● Sufficient exercise helps to reduce or eliminate common behavior problems such as digging, excessive barking, chewing, and hyperactivity.

● Exercise is a good way to help a timid dog build confidence and trust, because he will be socializing with other dogs and must be able to hold his own.

● Dogs need physical and mental stimulation every day. Exercise helps prevent boredom, and channels energy in a productive and acceptable direction.

● Exercise provides mental stimulation through territorial investigation. With his nose to the ground, your dog will gather information with all of his senses alert.

● Exercise helps to prevent depression in dogs in the same way that it helps people.

For both of you

Exercising together strengthens your bond and leads to increased trust and a deeper relationship. It provides motivation for you, because you know the benefits for your dog and want to give him the very best. Dogs make great exercise partners. They love to accompany their owners for a walk, jog, hike, swim, or game, and they won't hesitate to remind you when it's time for the daily romp.

What's more, simply owning a dog can encourage better health. Studies have shown

Above Getting your dog out and about is important to develop his socialization skills, and will offer vital mental stimulation.

that pet owners have measurably lower levels of cholesterol and blood pressure (where not linked to dietary changes) and a U.S. study found that men who own cats or dogs have lower resting heart rates and blood pressure than those who don't.

Your body shape

Being overweight doesn't necessarily mean being overfat. Many strong, healthy, and muscular people weigh much more than their overweight contemporaries and yet do not have an ounce of unhealthy fat on their bodies. Furthermore, your body shape and age can affect the way your weight is distributed and how much you weigh.

What shape are you?

Your body type is almost entirely determined by genetics and is therefore almost impossible to change, although you can build muscle or lose weight to shift extra padding or strengthen flabby areas, which will alter your overall silhouette. What's more, being fit means that you will look and feel your best, no matter what your shape. There are three main body types: ectomorph, mesomorph, and endomorph. Many people are a mixture of two body types. For example, a "meso-endomorph" might have a strong upper body, but have a tendency to put on weight on the lower part of the body.

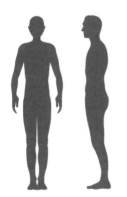

Ectomorphs are tall and thin with long limbs, small bones, and a narrow upper body. They aren't naturally muscular and have little fat storage.

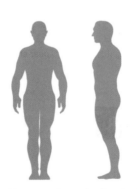

Mesomorphs tend to be short with broad shoulders, narrow hips, and well-developed muscles. They are low on body fat and gain muscle easily.

Endomorphs tend to be rounder with wide hips and large bones. They store fat easily and are prone to gaining weight.

Apples and pears

You may be a distinct body shape, but if your waist is larger than it should be, it could spell danger. Research shows that people with "apple-shaped" bodies (more weight around the waist) face more health risks than those with "pear-shaped" bodies (more weight around the hips). A 2005 study found that women who gain weight around their midsections are up to six times more likely to develop Type 2 diabetes than women who are pear-shaped.

Waist-to-hip ratio

It is now known that waist-to-hip ratio (WHR) is a better marker of cardiovascular disease than body mass index or BMI (*see pages 24–25*).

A study of 27,000 people from 52 countries was carried out to ascertain which measure of obesity (BMI, WHR, or waist or hip) shows the strongest relation to risk of cardiovascular disease. The study clearly showed that waist-to-hip ratio was the most accurate indicator.

Health risks based on WHR

	Male	Female
Low	0.95 or less	0.80 or less
Moderate	0.95–1.0	0.81–0.85
High	1.0 or higher	0.85 or higher

Which shape are you?

It's very easy to calculate your waist-to-hip ratio using a flexible measuring tape and a basic calculator:

1 Breathe out slowly. Don't hold your stomach in.

2 Measure your waist circumference at the narrowest part. Do not pull the tape too tight.

3 Measure your hip circumference at its widest part.

4 Divide waist measurement by hip measurement. For example, if your waist is 35 in and your hips are 41 in, then divide 35 by 41 and your calculator will give you a reading of 0.85. This is your waist-to-hip ratio.

5 If your WHR is higher than 0.85, you are apple-shaped. If it is lower, you are pear-shaped.

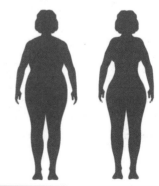

Your age

Growing older doesn't have to mean degeneration and the onset of age-related illnesses. Many studies show that a healthy lifestyle, including a good diet and regular, varied exercise, can keep problems at bay and actually slow down the aging process. However, it's worth considering that things won't always work the way they once did, and it's always sensible to take precautions.

Above An active lifestyle can help prevent problems as we get older.

Getting older

As we get older, many of us become less physically active. This is usually caused by a combination of age-related changes in our bodies, such as difficulty with movement and balance, decreased flexibility and stamina, aches and pains, and often the limitations of chronic diseases. Whatever the reasons, the result is a slowing down of our metabolism. If exercise raises the metabolic rate, it stands to reason that being less active will cause it to slow down. Unless we also reduce our caloric intake, weight gain is inevitable. This is true at any age, but is more likely to happen the older we get.

Less breath, fewer muscles

Among the age-related changes are those that affect the heart and lungs. Around the age of thirty, the functioning of these two vital organs begins to gradually decline. A similar decline takes place in muscle and bone mass. It is more difficult to increase muscle bulk, and

Left Keeping fit is essential for dogs and their owners, no matter what stage of life you are at. Even a short walk across local parkland will keep you active and benefit both of you.

bones begin to lose calcium, thus becoming thinner and more brittle. All of these changes can lead to a reduction in physical activity, unless you determine to maintain an active lifestyle and work at it every day.

The "change"

Women face an additional challenge because of hormonal shifts that occur as they approach and reach menopause. On average, women gain a pound a year from the age of thirty to the onset of menopause. This happens without any change in their eating or exercise habits. Many women find that their shape changes markedly as they begin to store more fat around the waist and belly. Exercise is crucial, not only because it helps to balance the hormones when performed regularly, but also because it can help to redistribute weight.

Not all bad news

Becoming, or remaining, physically active as you grow older is the best way to stave off the effects of aging. The good news is that exercise can boost metabolism, ensure that muscle mass is not lost, and keep your heart and lungs healthy. It is, however, important to take it slowly if you are older and haven't exercised for a while.

Aging doesn't necessarily deal us the best hand, but with regular effort we can do a great deal to turn back the clock, and our canine friends can join us as well.

Your dog's body

Dogs are a little bit more difficult to classify than people. The American Kennel Club divides dogs into seven groups: sporting, hound, working, terrier, toy, nonsporting, and herding. The body shapes differ enormously between these groups, as well as within them, as does musculature, weight distribution, and overall weight.

There are many other factors that affect your dog's body shape—for example, a large litter can mean smaller dogs—and there are often differences between the sexes and ages. It is important to recognize these differences. A large, active dog in the sporting group will undoubtedly look much leaner than an average toy. A Pug or a Bulldog can look heavy and yet be within a perfectly normal and healthy weight range, whereas an overweight Cocker Spaniel will be immediately recognizable.

Evaluating your dog's build

Don't rely too heavily on your dog's group when assessing his weight or his potential to undertake different types of activity. The Irish Wolfhound and the Dachshund are both members of the hound group, yet couldn't be more different. The American Kennel Club suggests that you evaluate your dog's structure on an individual basis.

Below It's much easier to assess overweight on a small dog with fine bones than a dog with a heavier-set physique. If in doubt, check with your vet.

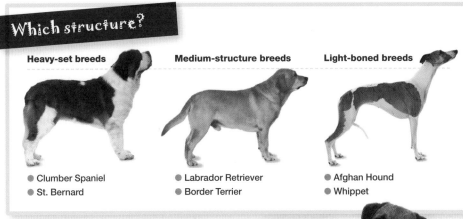

Which structure?

Heavy-set breeds

Medium-structure breeds

Light-boned breeds

- Clumber Spaniel
- St. Bernard

- Labrador Retriever
- Border Terrier

- Afghan Hound
- Whippet

The heavier a dog is in relation to his height, the more stress will be exerted on his musculoskeletal system. A Clumber Spaniel and an Afghan Hound may both weigh the same, but the Clumber Spaniel carries that weight on a smaller frame. More stress will therefore be exerted on his joints, bones, and muscles when he jumps and runs.

Just like people, the way a dog carries his weight and muscles on his bone structure can make some exercises more or less suitable.

Above Both old and young dogs are less prone to becoming overweight.

Age

Older dogs have slower metabolisms and are generally less active, which means that lean body mass can decline and extra fat can creep on. Dogs tend to become overweight between the ages of two and twelve, especially around the six-year mark. As dogs become more "senior," the tendency to become overweight decreases. Young dogs are also less likely to be overweight, because they are still growing and have higher energy requirements.

Your dog's body **23**

Are you overweight?

Many people underestimate their weight and tend to ignore the scale whenever possible. Although a head-in-the-sand approach can keep worries at bay, it will do nothing for your health. Let's look at the best ways to assess your weight—and determine whether you are over, under, or at a perfect weight.

Your body shape will define the distribution of your fat and muscles, and many perfectly healthy people will look heavier than others of the same weight because they are simply built that way. However, weight has a habit of creeping upward—a pound here, a pound there, and before you know it, you're ten pounds heavier than you used to be. That's why it's important to keep tabs on your weight and to find out where you stand on the scale.

Your BMI

Body Mass Index, or BMI, uses a mathematical formula that takes into account height and weight. It provides a reliable indicator of body fat for most people and is used to screen for weight categories that may lead to health problems.

The calculations are simple. Calculate your BMI by dividing weight in pounds (lb) by height in inches (in) squared (to the power of two) and multiplying by a conversion factor of 703.

Left It's worth weighing yourself on a regular basis, as an incentive to continue with your fitness plan, and to prevent things from spiraling out of control.

For example:

Weight = 150 lb
Height = 5' 5" (65 in)
Calculation: $150 \div (65)^2 \; [65 \times 65] \times 703 = 24.96$

BMI weight status

Below 18.5	**Underweight**
18.5–24.9	**Normal**
25.0–29.9	**Overweight**
30.0 and above	**Obese**

What does it mean?

For adults aged twenty years old and above, BMI is interpreted using standard weight-status categories that are the same for all ages and for both men and women.

The standard weight-status categories associated with BMI ranges for adults are shown in the table on the left.

Adding in waist size

The size of your waist, along with your BMI, is another indicator of overweight and, in particular, of health problems associated with overweight. This is shown in the table below.

Other ways of assessing overweight

Be realistic when you look at your body in a full-length mirror. Obvious rolls or handles of fat, an overhanging belly, and dimpled flesh are all signs of being overweight. "Pinching an inch" is also a good indicator. To do this, choose an area over your ribs and loosely hold the skin there between your thumb and forefinger. If there is more than 1 in (2.5 cm) of fat, there is too much!

Adding in waist size

BMI	Category	Men: waist 40 in (102 cm) or less Women: 35 in (89 cm) or less	Men: Waist greater than 40 in (102 cm) Women: greater than 35 in (89 cm)
18.5 or less	Underweight	N/A	N/A
18.5–24.9	Normal	N/A	N/A
25.0–29.9	Overweight	Increased	High
30.0–34.9	Obese	High	Very high
35.0–39.9	Obese	Very high	Very high
40 or greater	Severely obese	Extremely high	Extremely high

If your BMI is high, you may have an increased risk of developing many debilitating diseases.

Is your dog overweight?

It's clear that some dogs are naturally heavier-set and carry more fat than others, dependent upon breed and age; however, there is an easy way to assess whether or not your dog is overweight, and there are also broad guidelines to help you figure out whether there might be a problem.

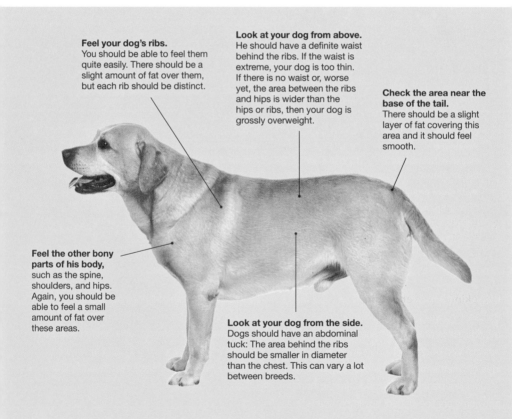

Feel your dog's ribs.
You should be able to feel them quite easily. There should be a slight amount of fat over them, but each rib should be distinct.

Look at your dog from above.
He should have a definite waist behind the ribs. If the waist is extreme, your dog is too thin. If there is no waist or, worse yet, the area between the ribs and hips is wider than the hips or ribs, then your dog is grossly overweight.

Check the area near the base of the tail.
There should be a slight layer of fat covering this area and it should feel smooth.

Feel the other bony parts of his body, such as the spine, shoulders, and hips. Again, you should be able to feel a small amount of fat over these areas.

Look at your dog from the side.
Dogs should have an abdominal tuck: The area behind the ribs should be smaller in diameter than the chest. This can vary a lot between breeds.

Which breed, what weight?

Here are some very general weight guidelines for popular breeds of dogs. If your dog's breed doesn't appear here, check the weight of the breed that is closest in size to your dog. If you still aren't sure, check with your vet.

● Small breeds

Chihuahua	4 lb (1.8 kg)
Pekingese	9 lb (4 kg)
Miniature Schnauzer	15 lb (6.8 kg)
Boston Terrier	19 lb (8.6 kg)

● Medium breeds

Cocker Spaniel	25 lb (11.3 kg)
Beagle	25 lb (11.3 kg)
Brittany Spaniel	35 lb (16 kg)

● Large breeds

Siberian Husky	50 lb (22.7 kg)
Airedale Terrier	50 lb (22.7 kg)
Pointer	65 lb (29.5 kg)
Labrador Retriever	75 lb (34 kg)

● Giant breeds

Old English Sheepdog	95 lb (43 kg)
Great Dane	130 lb (59 kg)
St. Bernard	165 lb (75 kg)

Checking for overweight

By checking several areas on your dog—the ribs, base of the tail, spine and shoulders, "waist," and abdomen—you can get a good idea of whether or not he is overweight.

Just like people, some dogs are big-boned and some are fine-boned, so simply checking the weight of an animal does not always provide enough information to make a sound assessment. For example, one Golden Retriever may be in fine shape at 85 lb (39 kg), whereas another could be overweight at 75 lb (34 kg).

The lifestyle questionnaires

Before making any changes, you will need to assess the lifestyles of both you and your dog, and focus on areas that need attention. Many of us consider our lives perfectly healthy until we notice that we've added a few extra pounds and routine daily activities feel like a chore. Read on to find out where your problem areas, and those of your canine companion, might be.

Your lifestyle

Check the answer to each question that most closely describes you.

1 How regular are your meals?

☐ **a** *You often skip them, especially breakfast.*

☐ **b** *You occasionally miss meals.*

☐ **c** *You have at least three meals a day.*

2 What do you usually eat for lunch?

☐ **a** *Fast food.*

☐ **b** *Sandwiches, potato chips, and cookies.*

☐ **c** *Freshly prepared food.*

3 How many portions of fruit and vegetables do you eat a day?

☐ **a** *Less than three.*

☐ **b** *Three or four.*

☐ **c** *Five or more.*

4 How often do you have carbonated drinks?

☐ **a** *Every day.*

☐ **b** *Three or four times a week.*

☐ **c** *Rarely.*

5 How often do you drink alcohol?

☐ **a** *Every night and more on weekends.*

☐ **b** *Two or three times a week.*

☐ **c** *Once a week or less.*

6 What do you usually do on weekends?

☐ **a** *Stay in and watch TV/DVDs.*

☐ **b** *Do household and gardening tasks.*

☐ **c** *Plan active day trips.*

7 What do you usually do in the evening or after work?

a *Go home and watch TV.*

b *Go out for dinner or a drink.*

c *Do an organized physical activity.*

8 How often do you exercise?

a *Rarely and intermittently.*

b *Two to three hours a week.*

c *Thirty to forty minutes every day.*

9 What makes you feel out of breath?

a *Walking up a flight of stairs.*

b *Running to catch a bus or train.*

c *Doing strenuous exercise.*

10 How do you lose weight if it is necessary to do so?

a *Take prescription diet pills.*

b *Go on a crash diet.*

c *Begin a regular exercise program.*

11 What do you do if you feel depressed?

a *Indulge in sweet or fatty treats.*

b *Lie around watching TV.*

c *Go for a long walk or bicycle ride.*

Your answers

If most of your answers are **As**, you are at risk for becoming overweight and related health problems. In a nutshell, your overall levels of nutrition, health, and fitness are substandard. Substantial changes need to be made to your leisure activities and eating habits, introducing nutritionally balanced meals and snacks.

If most of your answers are **Bs**, you are halfway to health problems. Too much of your diet is centered around unhealthy food, or food for comfort, and leisure activities are not always healthy enough to keep overweight and

ill-health at bay. Make some simple changes, such as those outlined later in this book, to prevent weight from becoming an issue in your life.

If most of your answers are **Cs**, keep on doing what you've been doing. Your overall approach to meal planning, nutrition, and fitness indicates a reduced risk of overweight and other health problems. Activity and exercise are integral parts of your life. Your concern about your own weight shows that you understand the need to be proactive and do all you can to maintain your health.

Your dog's lifestyle

Check the answer to each question that most closely describes your dog.

1 How does your dog behave at home?

☐ **a** He rarely moves from your side (or his dog bed).

☐ **b** He follows you around and plays.

☐ **c** He plays and is always desperate to get out.

2 How often does your dog snack?

☐ **a** Whenever he wants, including anything you snack on.

☐ **b** He is given a few treats during the day.

☐ **c** He is occasionally rewarded with a treat and rarely snacks.

3 How do you reward your dog?

☐ **a** By offering him unlimited treats.

☐ **b** By giving him occasional treats.

☐ **c** By taking him for an extra walk or play.

4 When does your dog have meals?

☐ **a** Whenever he is hungry.

☐ **b** About three times a day.

☐ **c** Once or twice a day, according to his size and weight.

5 What does your dog eat?

☐ **a** Dog food and anything going, including table scraps.

☐ **b** Dog food and suitable leftovers (see page 46).

☐ **c** High-quality dog food only and no table scraps.

6 How often does your dog exercise?

☐ **a** When you can manage it.

☐ **b** A few times a week for at least twenty to thirty minutes.

☐ **c** Every day, for at least thirty minutes.

7 What happens if your dog misses his daily walk?

☐ **a** He doesn't seem to notice.

☐ **b** He indicates that he'd like to go out.

☐ **c** He cajoles and begs until he gets you out the door.

8 How does your dog behave when exercising with you?

☐ a *He has difficulty keeping up and needs to rest frequently.*

☐ b *He mainly keeps up, but shows disinterest after a while.*

☐ c *He shows boundless energy and enthusiasm.*

9 What do you and your dog usually do together?

☐ a *Lie around watching TV and snacking.*

☐ b *Take a little exercise or play in the backyard.*

☐ c *Exercise actively for at least one hour a day.*

10 How does your dog appear physically?

☐ a *Overweight and slightly unkempt.*

☐ b *Healthy, but carrying a few too many pounds.*

☐ c *Lithe, strong, and healthy with a soft, shiny coat.*

11 How would you describe your dog's health?

☐ a *He has regular health problems and trips to the vet.*

☐ b *He is sometimes unwell, but mostly happy and healthy.*

☐ c *He is a picture of good health, regardless of his age.*

Your answers

Look back to page 29. The same holds true for dogs as much as humans. If most of your answers are **As**, you should be worried. Your dog is not eating healthily, has probably adopted some unhealthy habits, and rarely gets enough exercise. Remember, dogs are not in charge of their own health and well-being: you are!

If most of your answers are **Bs**, you are probably getting away with the bare minimum, but the truth is that this will eventually take its toll on your dog's health, in the form of overweight, health problems, and poor fitness.

If most of your answers are **Cs**, you are doing well. Your dog is eating healthily and you reward him appropriately. His exercise needs are a priority and you take time to meet them. You have a good, positive attitude, and your dog is probably a picture of robust canine health—something that a good diet and increased fitness can only continue to improve.

The program begins

Getting fit with your dog involves more than simply increasing the number of walks you share together. To achieve optimum health and well-being, and attain healthy levels of fitness, you'll need to address your whole lifestyle. This means ensuring that you are getting plenty of the right type of exercise, eating good-quality food, and looking after yourself. Starting any new fitness program also means considering your overall health, age, weight, and physical fitness, and taking the necessary precautions. Begin slowly, at a pace that is right for you, and gradually work your way toward finding a healthy balance.

Some breeds of dog, and older dogs, will have necessarily lower requirements, just as overweight dogs and their owners should take care to exercise gently at first, losing weight slowly and at a healthy rate. The goal is to achieve overall fitness, to get rid of those spare tires that may be affecting your health on all levels, and to increase your strength and vitality along the way. It doesn't take long to notice a big difference in the way you look and feel when you adopt the simple, enjoyable activities and advice given in this book. Choose the exercises that appeal the most to you and your dog, and that give you the most pleasure. This is an easy program to set you up for a healthier, happier lifestyle. So let's begin now.

Getting ready

There are some simple precautions that you will need to consider before beginning any exercise program, in order to protect yourself from injury and ensure that you and your dog are not taking unnecessary risks. Effective exercise is pleasurable, never painful, and it should fit neatly into your daily routine. Here's what to consider when starting out.

A good checkup

Before beginning the program, both you and your dog should pay a visit to your physician/veterinarian for a checkup. This will ensure there aren't any nagging health problems that should be addressed, or anything that might prohibit you from exercising regularly. This is particularly important if you or your dog are overweight or past middle age.

If you are both extremely unfit, and haven't had more than a jaunt between refrigerator and sofa for a while, you'll need to begin very slowly.

Beginning with ten minutes a day is a good start, and you'll soon work your way up slowly to optimum fitness levels.

Age

Some dogs and their owners are fit and energetic well into old age, and certainly healthier than some of their younger, overweight counterparts. However, age does bring with it a number of related health problems that can affect the ability to exercise. Older dogs will not be able to exercise for as long, and if they suffer from arthritis (or, in the case of some larger breeds, problems with their hips), you should take things slowly.

Caution!
Never feed a dog less than one hour before or after exercise, as her stomach may swell, causing gastric torsion. This can be fatal.

Left No matter how keen your dog might be to get started, it's always worth having him checked over by a vet to assess his fitness and overall health.

Keeping cool

All exercise, no matter how gentle, should be preceded by a warm-up and followed by a cool-down period (*see pages 58–59 and 102–103*).

Make sure your dog has access to plenty of fresh water while exercising, particularly in hot weather. Dogs overheat and dehydrate easily. Let your dog drink as often as she wants to. Similarly, you should drink regularly whenever you exercise.

Special cases

Puppies, which are still developing, older dogs, and pregnant bitches should not walk or run long distances. Any dog that has had an operation should not exercise until at least ten days after surgery. The same goes for you.

If you are pregnant, have had surgery, or fall into the "senior" category, check with your physician before beginning any program.

Setting the pace

Let dogs set their own pace, and when they appear tired (lying down or panting) then stop. Start with short bursts of exercise, and build it up slowly. If you feel tired, dizzy, or faint at any point, stop. Work up to the point where you feel challenged, but not beyond. A good test is if you can talk without gasping for breath. Exercise should never be painful. When it starts to hurt, stop. Watch out for signs that your dog might be uncomfortable. She'll stop running or playing, may pant a lot, yelp, or limp. Any of the above is a signal for you to stop.

Optimum nutrition for you

Whether you wish to lose weight or simply look and feel better, a healthy eating plan is the best place to start. This involves choosing your food carefully and creating a healthy balance of nutrients, while eating enough to sustain your new activity levels.

What's a healthy diet?

A healthy diet doesn't mean saying no to treats, or depriving yourself unnecessarily. It simply involves making better food choices, so that you have the energy you need to sustain a healthy lifestyle with plenty of exercise, as well as losing any unwanted pounds. No healthy diet is successful if it isn't sustainable, so the food you eat must be delicious, satisfying, easy to prepare, and practical. Even if you need to lose a lot of weight, you are better off increasing your exercise levels while changing your diet, rather than cutting down too much or too quickly. A realistic goal is to lose 1–2 lb (½–1 kg) a week.

Right If you base your daily meals around fresh fruit, vegetables, and herbs, you'll find it much easier to maintain your ideal weight and get all the nutrients you need.

The food pyramid

Research suggests that the pyramid structure works best to analyze and graphically show how our diets should be set up. It's obvious that the foods at the top of the pyramid are those that should be eaten less frequently, whereas those at the bottom can be consumed much more freely. Don't get hung up on portions, though.

The pyramid acts as a guide to help you understand which foods should be eaten most, and which should be considered treats, served irregularly and certainly not on a daily basis. And don't forget that the most important part of the pyramid is water. The body constantly loses water throughout the day and it must be replaced to prevent dehydration.

Other foods, *including candy, cookies, fast food, potato chips, and cake (not to be eaten on a daily basis, but okay as a very occasional treat)*

Proteins, *including very lean meats, fish, poultry, cheese, yogurt, nuts, soy products (including tofu), legumes such as lentils, and seeds (three to five servings a day)*

Fats and oils, *including butter, olive oil, unhydrogenated margarines, seed and nut oils (use sparingly; see page 38)*

Carbohydrates: *anything whole grain or unrefined, including pasta, bread, brown rice, grains (such as rye, barley, corn, wheat), legumes, potatoes, and whole grain, sugar-free cereals (four to nine servings a day)*

Fruit and vegetables and their juices: *anything goes. Remember that the more colorful the vegetable, the more nutritious it tends to be (five to ten servings a day)*

Fluids: *Water is the most important; 17–70 fluid ounces (500–2,000 ml) is recommended, depending on age and weather.*

Which fat?

Despite what you've heard, fat *is* necessary for overall health, and a deficiency may lead to cravings and health problems. Fat plays an important role in our bodies, and in older women it can help protect the bones.

Fats to avoid

Trans fats are produced through hydrogenation, a process that makes an unsaturated fat solid or spreadable, and are associated with heart disease and high cholesterol. Many packaged foods contain trans fats, but the good news is that the law now requires that fact to be listed on food labels.

Fats to eat sparingly

Saturated fats are found in animal products (including eggs, butter, cheese, and milk) as well as in some vegetable oils (coconut, palm, and palm-kernel). Eating too much saturated fat is one of the major risk factors for heart disease, high cholesterol, and overweight.

Fat in a healthy diet

A healthy, balanced diet (*see page 36*) will never include too much fat. It's the junk food and prepared meals that tend to be very high in saturated fats. It's also worth noting that if fats—even saturated fats—are eaten with plenty of fruit and vegetables in your diet, their impact is not as dangerous. The reason is that fruit and vegetables contain nutrients called antioxidants, which limit the damage that fat can do to your body.

Fats to eat more often

Unsaturated fats have the same number of calories as saturated and trans fats, but they have a wide range of benefits.

Monounsaturated fats have lower levels of unhealthy cholesterol and boost levels of healthy cholesterol. Monounsaturated fats include olive oil, sesame and peanut oils, avocados, nuts and seeds, and canola oil.

Polyunsaturated fats serve many functions, from lowering blood pressure and balancing blood sugar to maintaining the immune system.

They can be found in abundance in these oils: corn, cottonseed, flaxseed, grapeseed, safflower, sesame, soybean, and sunflower, as well as the blend usually labeled as vegetable oil. Other food sources are fish, eggs, nuts, seeds, whole grains, and green leafy vegetables. Polyunsaturated fats are also the source of omega-3, which plays a role in cell repair and brain development, and helps control cholesterol levels. The richest food source of omega-3 is oily fish such as herring, mackerel, salmon, sardines, and tuna.

A healthy balance

Your diet should be made up of a balance of fats (no more than 30 percent), carbohydrates, and protein. Fiber is also important for overall health and a balanced weight. If you emphasize unsaturated fats and complex carbs (see page 40), plus plenty of fresh fruit and vegetables, you'll get what your body needs.

Right Monounsaturated fats include olive oil, and sesame and peanut oils.

Think fresh

Look for fresh meat, eggs, cheese, yogurt, fish, and poultry rather than the processed versions. It's also important to get a balance of vegetable proteins, such as beans, nuts, seeds, legumes, grains, and even potatoes.

Carbs

Carbohydrates are energy food and the body's main source of fuel. There are two main types: refined and complex (unrefined).

Refined carbohydrates supply energy, but they are quickly assimilated, causing a sudden energy boost followed by a drop in energy. This results in mood swings, irritability, lethargy, and cravings. Refined carbohydrates have had the majority of their nutrients—including calcium, B vitamins, iron, zinc, and potassium—stripped by the refining process.

The message is to eat unrefined (complex) carbs, which have not been processed or refined. These supply a sustained source of energy, which means that it takes longer to digest and assimilate them. Unrefined foods contain vitamins, minerals, and proteins.

Protein

Protein helps to slow down the release of sugar from other foods into the bloodstream, which can have a big impact on your weight. Proteins are made up of different combinations of twenty-two separate amino acids, which our bodies need to function at every level. A lack of protein in the diet retards growth in children and causes a decrease in energy. So if you are feeling lethargic, a lack of high-quality protein may be part of the problem.

Know your carbs

Refined carbohydrates

White sugar and everything that contains it, including:
- Candy, cakes, and cookies
- Carbonated drinks
- Jams and jellies

White flour and everything that contains it, including:
- Bread and pasta
- Pies and crackers
- Breakfast cereals
- White rice

Unrefined (good) carbohydrates
- Fruit and vegetables (and their juices)
- Whole grain unrefined flour
- Whole grain pasta
- Brown rice
- Whole grain bread and cereals
- Oatmeal
- Legumes
- Whole grains, such as barley and quinoa

Suitable snacks

Try a little hummus with crudités; fresh fruit; fruit yogurts; a handful of nuts, seeds, or dried fruit; a slice of toast with banana or avocado; rice cakes; unsalted air-popped popcorn; a fresh fruit smoothie; or a little cheese.

Above Add zest to your diet by cooking creatively—use spices, herbs, and recipes from other cultures.

Snacks are on the menu!

Don't underestimate the importance of snacks. Regular, healthy snacks will help keep blood-sugar levels stable and prevent cravings and overeating at mealtimes. Stable blood-sugar levels mean that you won't experience the peaks and valleys that produce fatigue, ravenous hunger, and periods of low energy. Remember, however, that snacks are not treats, but another element of a healthy diet.

Regular meals

Beginning with breakfast, regular meals are essential to balanced weight and a healthy lifestyle. A 2003 study shows that those who skip breakfast have four-and-a-half times the risk of obesity of those who eat breakfast regularly. A 2005 study also found that eating regular meals encourages the body to deal more effectively with fats and carbohydrates, resulting in lower levels of fat in the blood and better metabolism of carbs, both of which can help prevent diabetes.

Aiming for optimum nutrition

Optimum nutrition involves eating high-quality, fresh foods, with plenty of healthy snacks. It also involves appreciating food—eating for the purpose of being healthy and active, and in order to get energy, rather than for the sake of it. You'll find that when you eat well, your cravings for sweet and fatty foods will diminish and be more easily satisfied. Drink plenty of fresh water each day to encourage healthy digestion and you'll soon find that your energy levels soar.

Doggie nutrition

Just like their owners, dogs need a balanced diet in order to attain optimum health and well-being. They also need to learn to enjoy healthy foods, and to avoid treats and other foods that may cause overweight and ill health.

What your dog needs

Optimum nutrition for your pooch includes a healthy balance of fats, carbohydrates, protein, fiber, vitamins and minerals, and water. This will ensure that your dog stays healthy and maintains a balanced weight.

Protein

Amino acids make up protein, and dogs, like humans, require them for growth, development, and energy. Good sources include meat, fish, poultry, eggs, and a little dairy.

Fats

Fats protect your dog's internal organs and provide insulation. Healthy fats, such as fish oils and nuts, keep your dog's coat lustrous, encourage a healthy metabolism, improve immune system functioning, and help with behavior, mood, and brain function. Excess fat, however, can lead to overweight and other health problems.

Right Rice and fresh vegetables are nutritious ingredients for healthy dog meals.

Carbohydrates and fiber

Carbohydrates produce energy and usually contain plenty of fiber. Rice, biscuit, wheat, corn, barley, and oats are all great for dogs. Fiber is not considered an essential nutrient in your dog's diet, but it is present in almost every commercial dog food. While dogs do not derive any energy from fiber, adding it to their diet improves colon health, assists with weight management, and helps prevent diarrhea, constipation, and diabetes. Some fiber is fermented into fatty acids (healthy fats) by the good bacteria in the intestine. These fatty acids will aid in preventing the growth of too much harmful bacteria in the intestine.

Vitamins and minerals

Minerals regulate body fluids, help form blood and bones, promote a healthy nervous system, and are essential for every bodily process. Many dog foods include mineral supplements. Dogs produce their own vitamin C in the liver, but they will need plenty of vitamins A, B, and E in order to keep them healthy.

Commercial dog foods contain between 30 and 70 percent carbohydrates; in the wild, however, a dog's diet would rarely contain more than 30 percent. So go easy on the carbs and include plenty of protein.

Water

All dogs need plenty of fresh water, offered frequently throughout the day. If your dog eats predominantly dry food, she'll need even more.

Which food?

Some experts recommend using only high-quality, complete dry foods, which contain optimum amounts of fats, carbohydrates,

Left Try making your own dog biscuits—a treat that is guaranteed to have only healthy ingredients.

protein, minerals, vitamins, and fiber. Dry foods keep well, are easy to store, and are more beneficial to your dog's teeth than canned food.

There are two types of canned food: one contains cereal and is a complete diet; the other is meat only and is designed to be fed in combination with dog biscuits. There may also be a difference in the amount of dog biscuits required to be fed per can, so be sure to read labels carefully before feeding your dog.

To feed a diet of canned meat only could lead to nutritional problems. Semi-moist diets come in the form of cubes or ground meat and provide a good alternative to canned food.

Another popular option is BARF—bones and raw food—which can be used instead of, or in addition to, commercially prepared dog food.

How much?

The amount of food a dog requires depends on its size and also on its age and daily exercise. Most commercially prepared dog foods include a feeding chart indicating the average food requirement by size of dog, and this will serve as a reasonable guide.

If there is a dramatic increase in the amount of exercise your dog gets, then she may need more food—even if the goal is to lose some weight. Check your dog's weight once a week. No dog should lose more than 1 lb (0.45 kg) for smaller breeds to 2 ¼ lb (1 kg) for larger breeds per week. If she's losing weight more quickly, you'll need to increase her food intake. Offer more dog biscuits and vegetables if your dog still seems hungry after her meals.

Above Dry dog foods contain optimum nutrition.

Table food

Most experts recommend that you not offer table food to your dog—largely because it tends not to be nutritionally balanced, and also because it is harder to control a dog's intake if she is constantly eating leftovers.

All dogs are different and some may require more food or a greater number of meals than others. You'll need to read the label on your regular pet food, but these tips will keep you on course:

● Puppies
Five small meals a day, reducing to four at three months, then three at eight months.

There are diets specifically designed for puppies and young dogs, which will ensure the growing dog receives the nutrition required for healthy growth.

● 12 months +
Two or more small meals a day.

Recent research has shown that even large breeds of dog are better fed two or more small meals a day, because this decreases the risk of gastric dilatation-volvulus or GDV (acute stomach bloat and torsion).

● Pregnant dogs
As much food as she wants to eat (provided she isn't overweight).

A pregnant dog's appetite will fluctuate, but she should be eating more in the latter stages of her pregnancy. If she is not, encourage her to eat more.

● Nursing bitches
Require much more food—up to two to four times their usual amount.

Allow your nursing bitch to eat as much as she pleases—let her hunger be your guide. Bitches with large litters may require even more.

● Older dogs
Two meals a day, but will probably eat less as their energy levels dip.

Watch out for energy-dense brands of dog food, which can contribute to overweight. Commercial adult dog foods will provide adequate nutrition.

Age considerations

As dogs age, they still need two meals a day, but will probably eat less as their energy levels dip. Dogs are defined as older or geriatric when they have reached the last 25 percent of their expected life span:

- Small-breed dogs older than twelve years
- Medium-breed dogs older than ten years
- Large-breed dogs older than nine years
- Giant-breed dogs older than seven years

Below If you have more than one breed, you may need to prepare different meals according to their needs.

Your dog's breed

Choose your dog's food carefully, according to her age, size, and breed. For example, some large-dog foods are lower in volume, but high in digestible protein, with additives that benefit a dog's joints. Dog breeds are generally divided into four categories at adult age:

Categories

small breeds	**20 lb (9 kg) or less**
medium breeds	**20–55 lb (9–25 kg)**
large breeds	**more than 55 lb (25 kg)**
giant breeds	**more then 100 lb (45 kg)**

● The smaller the breed, the greater the energy requirements per pound (0.45 kg) of weight. In general, a 10 lb (4.5 kg) dog will need about 60 percent more food than a 35 lb (16 kg) dog.

● Nordic breeds of dog (Siberian Huskies, Samoyeds, Alaskan Malamutes) enjoy a better-than-average energy return and therefore have energy needs that are approximately 20 percent lower than other breeds.

● Certain breeds predisposed to obesity, such as Labrador Retrievers and Beagles, may require about 10 percent less food.

What about snacks?

Dogs do not need snacks between meals. If you give your dog treats, make sure you take this into consideration when feeding; in other words, reduce the number of dog biscuits or amount of kibble according to what she has already been given in the form of treats. If your dog is accustomed to food rewards, try to switch to healthier alternatives, such as bits of carrot or apple, or a light biscuit. Try making your own dog biscuits, which tend to be lower in fat, unhealthy preservatives, and additives. Obviously, while you are training your dog, you may need to rely on treats to achieve the desired result, and to reward your dog. However, use them sparingly and ensure that you give her smaller meals later in the day.

Some adult dogs do not have sufficient amounts of the enzyme lactase, which breaks down the lactose in milk. This deficiency can result in diarrhea. Lactose-free milk products are available.

Make your own dog biscuits

Veggie Bites

This is a good way to increase vegetables in your dog's diet, provide fiber, vitamins, and minerals, and satisfy a doggie sweet tooth.

3 cups whole grain flour

*⅓ cup powdered milk
(lactose-free or soy is fine)*

¼ cup wheat germ

*½ cup puréed vegetables
(such as peas, green beans, zucchini, carrots, or even fruit such as apples)*

½ cup vegetable oil

¼ cup water

Place the flour, milk, and wheat germ in a mixing bowl. Add the veggie purée and oil, and blend well. Add water to make a stiff dough. Place the dough on a floured surface and roll out about ½ in (1.2 cm) thick. Cut out shapes with a cookie cutter. Bake at 350°F (180°C) for thirty minutes, or until firm. Allow to cool.

Starting out

If you haven't exercised in a while, it's important to start slowly and gradually build up. Everyone needs roughly the same amount of exercise each day to stay fit; however, if you take it at your own pace, you will still achieve the desired results over time.

What you need

There are several different types of exercise that everyone needs in order to be fit.

Aerobic

Aerobic exercises get your heart and lungs working while exercising other muscles as well. It's the best exercise for weight loss because it encourages a healthy metabolism and actively burns calories. Jogging, walking, swimming, cycling, and dancing are all aerobic.

Flexibility

These exercises stretch the muscles and extend the body's various bending points to achieve greater mobility, reduce the risk of muscle strain, and improve balance. Stretching is an important part of warming up and cooling down before exercising. Bending, throwing a ball, swimming, yoga, and agility courses can all make you more lithe and mobile.

Resistance (strength)

Any activity that involves lifting, pulling, or pushing against something is a resistance exercise, designed to build muscle strength. Most gym equipment is designed for this purpose, but gardening and many household chores also offer good resistance exercises. So do climbing stairs, exercises such as push-ups and sit-ups, and cycling, rowing, and swimming.

Left Your dog may be fitter than you so make sure you take the lead and exercise at your own pace.

How much?

For good cardiovascular fitness you should exercise three to five times a week, for between thirty and sixty minutes. The main concern is to ensure that your heart and lungs are worked hard enough and long enough to gain the benefits of aerobic exercise, but not for so long that you risk injury. To check whether you are exercising at the correct intensity, you should be slightly out of breath, but still capable of speaking.

Starting your program

It is important to start a new program slowly. If a thirty-minute session feels like too much, start with ten-minute sessions for the first week then increase them to fifteen- or twenty-minute sessions the next week, and so on until you feel comfortable exercising for longer.

Begin with walking

For the first few weeks of your program, in which you move from a sedentary lifestyle to one that is more active, you should gradually increase the number of steps you take each day. Strap on a pedometer and note your current step average over three days. For the first week, try to increase your number of steps by 25 percent. If you are currently walking 4,000 steps a day, work toward 5,000 steps in the first week, then 6,250 the next, and so on. It may take a few weeks to build up to an ideal 10,000 steps a day, but a slow and gradual buildup is the ideal way to begin.

Listen to your heart

Aerobic exercise should not raise your heart rate to more than 75 percent of your heart's maximum capacity. To estimate your maximum heart rate (MHR), subtract your age from 220. Ideally, your aerobic rate should reach a point between 50 and 75 percent of your MHR and stay there for twenty minutes or more.

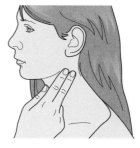

Not sure how to begin? Choose an artery in your neck or wrist and use your middle and index finger to find your pulse. Count the beats for 15 seconds and then multiply by four to get your beats per minute. This is your heart rate and it can be measured regularly as you exercise to find how close you are to your maximum.

Increasing the pace

After three or four weeks of increasing the number of steps you take each day, you'll undoubtedly notice a difference in the way you feel and what you are able to achieve. Now it's time to take your program further, to get a balance of the three different types of exercise (*see pages 48–49*).

Try to push yourself a little further every day—even an extra minute or two added to your regular exercise routine can make a difference.

Weightlifting

Carry a can of beans (or dog food) in each hand while you walk or jog; this not only increases the aerobic effect, but also helps to strengthen your upper body. Later in the book you'll find some good resistance exercises to try while your dog is busy elsewhere.

1 Experiment with intensity. If you are up to thirty minutes a day walking, try to jog for two to three minutes of that, or to walk quickly for five minutes, return to slower walking, then walk briskly again for another five minutes.

2 Continue to increase your weekly steps (*see page 49*) by 25 percent, until you reach the magic "healthy" recommendation of 10,000 steps per day.

3 Add time to your walks. Adding an extra five minutes or so per week can make a big difference to overall fitness. Strive for five thirty- to forty-minute walks per week by the end of the second month.

Incorporating other exercise

The key is to balance the three different types of exercise, focusing mainly on aerobic exercise for overall health and fitness. Throughout this book you'll find plenty of games and activities that will increase your flexibility and provide resistance to build muscle mass without you even knowing it!

In the beginning, focus on aerobic exercise with some walking, moving on to brisk walking and then jogging. Incorporate some fetch-and-carry games (*see pages 74–77*) in order to maximize your flexibility.

Add variety

Try some of these ideas to add variety to your routine. Not only will you ensure that you are getting a good balance of exercise, but the variety will help prevent boredom:

● Make one of your daily sessions a brisk walk, another a slow walking jog, and another a hike on uneven terrain.

Jogging is great for weight loss and aerobic exercise, but can be hard on the joints. Rollerblading burns a comparable number of calories, but is considered "low impact," which is easier on the joints.

● Take your dog for a swim in the local pond, or for a bike ride around the park.

● Consider a session of inline skating or roller skating, or even try an agility course (*see pages 92–93*) alongside your dog.

Below Throwing is great for flexibility, and can make you more lithe and mobile.

Doggie beginners

All dogs require exercise and play, in order to achieve a healthy level of fitness and to be happy, agreeable pets. It's important, however, to take into consideration your dog's individual needs before beginning a program—and remember to start off slowly.

If your dog has been inactive for some time, or is in her very junior or senior years, you may notice that she finds it difficult to keep up. Never push your dog beyond what feels comfortable for her. If she's panting a lot or stopping to rest, slow down and make sure she has a break and plenty of fresh water to drink.

The plan outlined for you on page 48 is perfect for your dog to begin with. Walking, even briskly, and increasing your steps each week, is suitable for almost any healthy dog, with the exception of some toy breeds, which may not be able to keep up. Walking offers these benefits for your dog:

- Aerobic exercise
- Freedom to play
- A natural way to stretch, encouraging flexibility
- Socialization with other dogs
- Essential sensory stimulation

Playtime

Alongside your walking targets, encourage your dog to play by bringing along a favorite toy or a ball (*see pages 78–81*). Running, leaping, catching, and retrieving are all excellent forms of exercise for your dog, improving strength, lung and heart capacity, flexibility, and even temperament.

Left Many small dogs have high exercise requirements. Make sure you know what your dog needs.

Exercise requirements

● Minimal exercise requirements

Cavalier King Charles Spaniel | Miniature Pinscher | Pekingese
Pug | Toy Poodle

● Low exercise requirements

Basset Hound | Beagle | Bearded Collie
Bichon Frise | Boston Terrier | Chihuahua
Corgi | Dachshund | English Bulldog
French Bulldog | Greyhound | Jack Russell Terrier
Lhasa Apso | Miniature Poodle | Pomeranian Terrier
Shih Tzu | West Highland Terrier | Yorkshire Terrier

● Medium exercise requirements

Afghan Hound | Airedale Terrier | Alaskan Malamute
American Bulldog | Border Terrier | Borzoi
Boxer | Bull Terrier | Cairn Terrier
Chow Chow | Cocker Spaniel | Collie
Dalmatian | Fox Terrier | German Shepherd
Giant Schnauzer | Golden Retriever | Great Dane
Great Pyrenees Mountain Dog | Irish Wolfhound | Labrador Retriever
Miniature Schnauzer | Old English Sheepdog | Pointer
Rhodesian Ridgeback | Rottweiler | Saint Bernard
Staffordshire Bull Terrier | Standard Poodle | Standard Schnauzer
Weimaraner | Whippet

● High exercise requirements

Australian Cattle Dog | Australian Shepherd | Border Collie
Bullmastiff | Doberman | English Setter
Gordon Setter | Husky | Irish Setter
Newfoundland | Shetland Sheepdog | Springer Spaniel

Who wants more?

Your dog will soon let you know when she's ready for more and different forms of exercise. Then it's a natural progression to the intermediate plan, where variety and plenty of different types of exercise will result in ever-improving health and fitness.

Above Take advantage of your dog's natural enthusiasm to introduce different types of exercise.

You may find that your dog is ready to progress more quickly than you are. If she still seems eager to carry on when you've reached your limit, there are many ways for her to be more active while you continue at a steady pace.

Add variety

Try some of the following to spice up your dog's exercise routine and move her easily and efficiently onto the next stage of the program:

- Games can easily be incorporated into your dog's daily exercise—bring along something for her to fetch and return to you.
- If there is a pond, lake, or gently flowing stream in your local park, encourage her to swim to retrieve a toy or a ball (*see page 76*).
- Set up an agility course (*see page 83*) in your backyard, and encourage her to master it—exercising two or three times a week for twenty or thirty minutes in between walks.
- Change the terrain. Your dog will use up far more energy (and burn off more calories), while building muscle and becoming more flexible.

Above Your dog should get at least thirty to sixty minutes of aerobic activity a day to maintain health and fitness levels.

• Give your dog the opportunity to run beside you when you cycle or inline skate. Safety measures must be employed (*see pages 94–97*), but this will give your dog a good all-around workout.

• Encourage your dog to jump for toys (where there is a safe landing area) to raise her heart rate and encourage flexibility.

Exercise targets

To maintain good health and overall fitness, try to ensure your dog has:

• at least thirty to sixty minutes of aerobic activity, such as running, walking, jogging, and fetching, every day.

• at least twenty to thirty minutes of agility training or games two or three times a week.

Ask a neighbor

If your dog has more energy and time than you do, consider asking a neighborhood child to take her for that extra walk or play session.

And if your dog still seems eager for more, introduce a regular playtime in your backyard, local park, or even inside the house, where fetch-and-carry games (*see pages 74–77*) can be combined with quick runs up and down the stairs.

Always tailor your dog's program to her individual needs. If she seems tired, slow down and offer plenty of rest; if she's restless and pulling on the leash, give her freedom to run and explore on her own. This will encourage her to meet her optimum fitness levels and satisfy her natural desire to explore her environment.

Combining your programs

Most healthy dogs can take part in a variety of activities, and you can easily tailor your dog's fitness plan to work with your own. The secret is to plan carefully to ensure that both you and your dog are motivated and getting maximum enjoyment from your time together.

Some forms of human exercise are obviously not suitable for dogs, such as going to the gym, swimming in a recreational pool, and, in some cases, inline skating or cycling, which can be too much for smaller or very old or young dogs. However, that doesn't mean you can't both get what you need with some careful planning. Here are some effective ways to join your fitness programs together.

In the park

This is a natural playground for dogs, with plenty of opportunities for you to work out as well:

● Encourage your dog to run, jump, fetch, and play with a toy or ball while walking or jogging yourself. Bending, throwing, and reaching all provide great toning, stretching, and strengthening exercises for you, too.

● Warm-ups and cool-downs should be practiced by you both, so encourage her to do a little stretching alongside you (*see page 59*) to develop flexibility and prevent injuries.

● Strap on your pedometer and encourage your dog to keep up with your ever-increasing steps.

Out and about

Go hiking and take long-distance walks when you have more time. Most dogs will benefit from uneven terrain and enjoy the opportunity to explore a new environment. Take along plenty of water and food, but make sure your dog doesn't exercise for at least thirty minutes after eating.

In the backyard

Set up an agility course that you can both use (*see page 82*). A course can easily be set up in your backyard, local park, or other green space and will have benefits for you both.

- Crawling through a tunnel, for example, provides resistance exercise for both of you.
- Running between obstacles offers a cardiovascular workout.
- Climbing and jumping tone, strengthen, and stretch the body.

Encourage your dog to play with toys—fetching, carrying, and jumping—when she's ready to go and you need a break.

Above An agility course with a tunnel provides effective resistance exercise.

Your goal

You may find that your dog needs more exercise than you do as she becomes fitter; alternatively, you may realize that an older or smaller dog can't keep up with you all the time. If this is the case:

- Engage in some stretching exercises while your dog bounds about at the park, or have a rest while she explores her environment.

- Allow her to rest with a bowl of water while you do some jogging in place or walk a short distance away.

- Pep up her routine with some running around and play in the backyard while you relax and sip a cold drink.

As long as both of you are getting at least thirty minutes of exercise every day, of all kinds, you will have achieved your goal.

Warming up

Warming your muscles with some gentle stretching is the best way to start any exercise routine, because stretching helps prevent injuries, increases your range of motion, releases muscle tension that can lead to cramping or pulls, and keeps oxygenated blood moving around the body.

Before beginning any daily exercise, you'll need to warm up. Start by walking for five minutes at a comfortable pace for you and your dog, swinging your arms gently as you go, raising them above your head, and bending every few steps to reach toward your toes. Don't bounce or overstretch to the point of pain, but give your limbs a good pull, within your comfort level.

Reach for the skies

Stretch your arms above your head and extend your fingers as far as you can. Turn your palms upward and join your fingers together. Stretch and hold for fifteen seconds, then repeat.

Above Precede all forms of exercise with stretching to maximize the effects and prevent injuries.

Calf lunges

Place your hands on your hips and one foot several inches in front of the other. Bend your front leg to stretch the calf muscle of your rear leg, keeping both heels on the ground. Hold for fifteen seconds and change legs.

Hamstring stretch

Sit with one leg bent out to the side and the other straight in front of you. Reach forward slowly, bending from your hips, until you are as far as possible over your outstretched leg. Keep your head upright. Hold for fifteen seconds and change legs.

Swivel those hips

Circle your hips in ever-greater movements to loosen them before a walk, pushing your pelvis forward and back in a circular movement for thirty seconds. Change direction and repeat.

Caution!

Avoid stretching with overweight, unfit, or arthritic dogs because it will cause them great discomfort.

Stretch your pooch

Dogs don't actually need to stretch to the same extent as people, because they naturally flex and stretch their muscles and joints on their own. However, a warm-up will loosen muscles and help prevent injuries. Many dogs enjoy stretching, especially if they are fit and agile with an even temperament.

1 Hold her front paws firmly and raise them so that she is standing on her back legs, pulling gently upward until she is almost vertical. This will release tension in her back and legs.

2 Place yourself behind your standing dog and gently pull her legs straight out behind her, so that her back is gently bent. See the muscles tighten and loosen along the length of the body.

3 Gently massage the muscles around her joints, and pull her legs carefully to loosen them.

Walking

Perhaps the simplest and most obvious of activities you can enjoy with your dog, walking is nonetheless an excellent option for you both, working on many levels to help you achieve optimum health and fitness.

Why walk?

Don't underestimate how effective walking can be. Studies show that for both dogs and their owners, walking can do the following:

- Reduce the risk of heart disease and strokes
- Lower blood pressure
- Reduce high cholesterol
- Reduce body fat
- Enhance mental well-being
- Reduce the risk of Type 2 diabetes
- Increase bone density, thereby helping to prevent osteoporosis
- Reduce the risk of cancer of the colon
- Encourage healthy sleep patterns
- Improve self-esteem, relieve symptoms of depression and anxiety, and improve mood
- Help to control body weight
- Encourage flexibility and coordination, which reduces the risk of injury and falls
- Help to achieve a longer life

Above Most dogs will remind their owners when it is time for a walk—perfect motivation to get out and do some exercise.

How much?

For general health, it is recommended that you walk briskly for at least thirty minutes per day, every day of the week. However, even a ten-minute brisk walk can increase fitness levels. One study found that women walking continuously for thirty minutes, five days per week, had an increase in fitness almost identical to that of women who split their thirty minutes into three ten-minute walks. Encouragingly, short-walkers lost more weight and reported greater decreases in waist circumference than the long-walkers did.

Even if you get very little other exercise, walking can improve your health and fitness on all levels. Walking is also the ideal exercise for dogs, who should be able to meet your own targets with ease and become fitter as you do.

What intensity?

The intensity of walking for fitness benefits varies according to your age and fitness level, but in general, "brisk is best." A simple way to figure out how briskly you should walk is to aim to walk "fast without overexertion." You should be able to hold a conversation while you are walking (the "talk test"). Your dog should be enjoying the walk and not panting or stopping to rest repeatedly (see page 55).

Above An enthusiastic dog might push you faster than you like. If it's safe to do so, let her off the leash while you set your own pace.

Walking 1 mile (1.6 km) can burn at least 100 calories of energy, and walking 2 miles (3.2 km) a day, three times a week, may help reduce weight by 1 lb (0.45 kg) every three weeks.

Above Walking on different surfaces makes your muscles work harder and has great aerobic benefits.

Which terrain?

All walking is good for you, but walking on uneven terrain targets your legs, buttocks, and thigh muscles, as well as providing even greater aerobic benefits. Because you have to lift your feet higher and make small adjustments to your movements, this increases your calorie expenditure by up to 26 percent compared with even-terrain walking. What's more, the variation in surfaces encourages your muscles and brain to work together to adapt to the challenges, which helps with mental acuity as well.

But don't worry if your only local terrain is a grassy park, an even path, or just the sidewalk.

Every step counts. The important thing is to increase your pace regularly so that you become more efficient. As you increase your steps, you should not, in fact, be spending much more time on your regular walks. You should become naturally faster.

Added resistance

For added resistance on your walks, you and your dog can try the following:

● Walk on different surfaces, such as sand, shallow water, fallen leaves, long grass, or even snow. This makes different muscles work harder, producing a more effective workout and increasing your strength.

● Use obstacles while you are out and about (such as benches, trees, ditches, and logs) to balance on (which will improve coordination and flexibility) and also for your dog to jump over or crawl under.

Use your body

To enhance the benefits of walking, it makes sense to use as many muscle groups as possible. Your dog has the ability to exercise her whole body, using all four legs to walk. You, however, may need to work a little harder:

● Bend your arms at 90-degree angles and pump them from your shoulders as you go. Moving them to keep pace with your legs will help you burn up to 10 percent more calories than walking with your arms at your sides.

- When you have your dog on a leash, leave a small amount of slack or use a retractable leash that is free of any snags and flows freely to and from the receptacle.
- Lift your legs higher—if you can't find rugged terrain, then imagine it. Lift your legs and feet as high as possible, as if you are marching.
- Let your dog "walk you." Let her lead and be sure to keep up with her pace as she scrambles over objects, races around corners, stops to check a scent, chases a squirrel, or pulls on her leash to go farther and faster. This doesn't mean allowing her to pull you on your walk (*see page 69*), but rather to set the pace. You may find she's the best personal trainer you'll ever have!

(*see page 69*)

Caution!

Wherever possible, choose routes that keep you and your dog away from speeding vehicles. If you must walk along a busy road, ensure that you are facing the traffic, with your dog on the inside. At every street corner, encourage your dog to stop and sit, which teaches her to wait before crossing the road. It may be time-consuming, but it's also likely to save her life if she goes off on her own.

Below Letting your dog set the pace sometimes will give you a more thorough workout.

Long-distance walking

Long walks or hikes cannot always be arranged in a busy schedule, but if you have some free time, the benefits for both you and your dog are enormous. Fresh air in unspoiled countryside will be a treat for you both, and will help you work your way to fitness.

Do your planning! Not all parks, woodlands, or fields are dog-friendly, nor are dogs allowed everywhere. Find out if there are any restrictions.

Slowly does it

Both you and your dog will need to be ready before you embark on long walks or hikes, or walk on unfamiliar terrain. Work up to it slowly, walking for increasing distances and stopping when you both feel tired. Practice on local wooded land, so that your dog becomes used to the terrain and to distractions. When you are both conditioned, you will be able to attempt longer walks together.

On the leash

All dogs benefit from being off the leash for short periods, to run and play without being controlled. However, in unfamiliar places, dogs should be kept on a leash at all times, particularly in the woods. While it may be tempting to set her free when there are few others about, keeping her on a 4–6 ft (1.2–1.8 m) leash will help her to stay out of trouble, keep her out of the way of others, and protect her from potential predators, such as hunters or wild animals. If you must let your dog off the leash,

Caution!

• If your dog gets a cut or scrape, you'll need to clean the injury and call a halt to the walk.

• Keep your dog's nails properly clipped to avoid tearing or pulling injuries caused by uneven terrain.

make sure that she stays within your field of vision and that you have good voice command recall—and it must be effective, even if your dog is in the throes of a successful chase.

Above Spending a day out with your dog is a great bonding experience, and provides an excellent opportunity for exercise.

Food

Nutrition is another consideration in training your dog. A complete and balanced diet will enable your dog to keep her energy up during a hike or long walk. Bring along plenty of healthy snacks, such as vegetables, dog biscuits, or a meal if you are going to be out for some time—but make sure that your dog has digested her meal before undertaking heavy exercise. High-density snacks, such as nuts, seeds, dried and fresh fruit, whole grain sandwiches, and even cold pasta salads, will provide energy for you.

Water breaks

Water is essential for both you and your dog; both of you should drink as much and as often as you wish. Pond water isn't any healthier for your dog than it is for you. You can teach your dog to drink from a squirt bottle, or bring along a collapsible water dish. If your dog seeks out shady spots, pants excessively, or if her gums become red, stop and cool her down. Gently pour water on her stomach and groin, too.

Below Don't hesitate to invest in a set of boots for your dog if you walk regularly on uneven or very hot terrain.

Watch those paws

On very uneven terrain, a dog's paws can become sore. It's not uncommon for dogs to sustain injuries to their footpads when hiking, particularly in the woods or on rocky terrain, which can cut and scrape the feet. While it's difficult to choose the terrain you walk on, you can purchase all-terrain boots for dogs who are exercising on extremely rough ground, in woodlands, or on snow or ice.

Choose your own footwear carefully, too. Ankle support is essential on uneven terrain. There should also be good padding to protect your feet and a firm exterior to prevent injuries.

Caution!

After any hike, check carefully for ticks, other insects, burrs, or thorns in your dog's coat. Watch out for signs of encounters with stinging nettles, poison oak, or ivy.

Heat and cold

In high or very low temperatures, you'll need to keep an eye out for heat exhaustion or hypothermia in your dog and ensure, too, that you are appropriately dressed. Chances are that your dog will have a better resistance to cold than you ever will, but if you live in a snowy climate it is necessary to purchase some doggie boots to protect her paws from snow, ice chips, and salt, which can get between the toes and cause infection or injury. If your dog is thin, you might want to invest in a warm coat.

Dogs are often ill-equipped to deal with high temperatures, and do not sweat in the same way that humans do. It is therefore important to keep hot-weather walks to a minimum, choosing the early morning or evening when it is cooler, and sticking to surfaces that do not hold the heat, such as grass or dirt paths.

How much walking?

As long as you are both comfortable and take time for regular rests, in between bouts of keeping your heart rate at an optimum level (*see page 49*), you can walk for as long as you wish. A couple of hours is a good starting hike for conditioned "beginners."

Who's got the bags?

Dogs can carry their own weight on a hike, or at least part of it. A healthy dog ought to be able to carry up to one-third of its weight in a special dog pack. Start with an empty pack with a few newspapers to acclimatize your dog to the pack, before you gradually increase the weight on successive hikes. Don't expect your dog to carry a pack on a hot, sunny day because it may cause her to overheat.

Right Invest in a doggie backpack so she can carry her own food and water—and perhaps yours too!

Jogging

While humans are better suited to jogging than are many dogs, establishing a regular running routine, allowing your dog to make pit stops and take sniffing breaks along the way, is a good way to encourage overall aerobic fitness.

When your walks are easily mastered and you've hit the magic 10,000 steps or higher (*see page 49*), you may feel ready to move on to jogging. Take it slowly, particularly if your exercise sessions tend to take place on a "binge" basis and you aren't used to regular activity. If you and your dog can walk briskly for twenty to thirty minutes without tiring, you can work up to a jog.

The best way to begin is to pick up your walking pace until it reaches a slow jog, and continue for as long as possible. If you start to feel uncomfortable or too breathless to speak, you've probably reached your maximum capacity for the moment. Slow down to a brisk walk and wait until your heart rate is within normal bounds (*see page 49*).

Just like you, your dog will need to build up to jogging, with short running sessions interspersed with her regular walks and foraging activities.

Left Jogging isn't for everyone as it's a high-impact activity. But if you are up to it, your dog will undoubtedly join you.

Right A trained dog is a safe dog. Keep her on a close leash when there are other dogs or potential dangers about.

Is your dog trained?

Make sure you teach your dog how to heel. Keeping your dog at your side while jogging is essential. If she lurches ahead or drags behind you when you walk at a leisurely pace, imagine the problems that can occur when you're moving at higher speed. Constantly pulling on your dog can damage her throat as well as throw you off balance.

In addition, teach your dog to sit and stay. This is essential for those times when you need to stop at intersections and at the approach of bicyclists, dogs, other joggers, darting squirrels, and any other potential distractions along narrow jogging trails and other bottleneck-type areas.

Your dog will soon understand that when you set out at a pace, she isn't in for a leisurely walk, or that when you pick up your bicycle, she's expected to keep up. Encourage her with lavish praise when she does match your pace, and she'll be more likely to continue to do so.

Jogging dogs

Jogging is not suitable for all breeds:
• Small dogs with short legs should not be walked or jogged for as long as larger dogs.
• Breeds with short noses may have trouble breathing when exercised vigorously. Short-snouters range from little Pugs to Bulldogs, Boxers, and many others.
• Don't assume that racing breeds such as Greyhounds and Whippets can keep up the pace. Although they are built to run fast, they were not bred to run for long distances.
• For young pups and big breeds of any age, sustained jogging or running is too hard on the joints. Short bursts may be okay, but let your dog set the pace.

Be careful!

Remember, dogs will usually try to keep up with their owners just because it is in their nature to do so. This can mask fatigue and overshadow signs that your dog is overdoing it. So be vigilant and do not push your dog too hard.

Footwear matters

Check out your dog's footpads after you return from jogging, and during your jog if your dog shows any change in gait or pace. Some surfaces, such as gravel and rock, can be very hard on dogs' feet. Check the pads for cracking or signs of wear. Watch out for glass shards and debris; remember, you have footwear, but your canine usually does not.

Your own footwear should be designed for running, walking, or cross-training. According to the American Orthopedic Foot and Ankle Society, a good running shoe has a soft upper,

plenty of cushioning for shock absorption, and a rocker sole that encourages the natural roll of your foot during jogging or walking.

Ask for a half size bigger than you normally take, allowing wiggle room for your toes. Your heel should, however, fit snugly into the back of the shoe. If shoes feel even remotely uncomfortable, don't buy them.

Your goal

Begin with interval training, which means alternating short periods of hard work with short recovery periods. Intervals will help you to get fitter and faster at jogging. Once you've warmed up (*see pages 58–59*), start with a brisk walk, increase the pace to a slow jog, and then intersperse faster bursts of running with more moderate recovery periods. Try alternating one minute at a faster pace with ninety seconds at a slower pace to recover.

You may not always be able to jog with your dog, so swap a bit of your time for a backyard play session, and leave her to her own devices while you take a jog around the park. Work up to forty-five minutes once a week, or do two thirty-minute sessions on alternate days.

On the leash

Training your dog to run with you, as opposed to pulling you, is vital for safety reasons. Leash options vary from harnesses to a hands-free dog-jogging leash, which clips on to a belt. Try to keep your dog no more than 6 ft (2 m) from you at all times, to prevent tangling and accidents with the leash, and to ensure that she doesn't get caught up in a game of chase-the-squirrel instead of focusing on the job in hand.

Top tips for jogging

Taking a few precautions can keep your dog safe and healthy while you exercise:

• Make sure your dog has an ID tag incase you get separated.

• Always check with your vet before starting your dog on any running program.

• Keep your dog's toenails trimmed to avoid snagging them on twigs or branches.

• Carry plenty of water and offer it to your dog frequently. However, never force her to drink.

• Never run in the heat of the day. Dogs dehydrate faster than humans.

• If your dog is panting heavily, or listing from side to side, slow down to a gentle walk.

• If you jog at night, wear reflectors and attach one to your dog's collar.

• Avoid jogging on a full stomach—both of you!

• Ensure that dogs are allowed in the areas where you choose to exercise—some parks, swimming holes, and even woodlands or nature reserves do not allow dogs, even on a lead.

Moving onward

Once you've started losing weight and feeling the benefits of a regular exercise plan, there is no doubt that you'll feel motivated to continue. The benefits to you and your dog will be obvious—a closer relationship, healthier weight, and increased fitness and well-being on all levels.

There will always be times when you don't feel up to the task, or when circumstances overtake the hours you have free to exercise; you may reach a plateau and find that the weight is not dropping off quite so quickly, or that your exercise routine has become boring. The secret is not to give up. Plateaus are effectively breathing spaces, giving the body a chance to adjust, and after a couple of weeks you'll find that your enthusiasm returns to normal.

Adding some variety to your exercise program, and gearing it into maintenance mode, are positive steps toward achieving your final goal. Exercise must be fun for it to become a part of your daily lifestyle and for you to feel inspired to continue. You may find that a daily walk or run with your dog isn't as stimulating as it used to be, and that you are both eager for new challenges. Exciting ball games, agility training (which you can get involved in, too!), or workouts on wheels or in the water may be just what you need to get your enthusiasm flowing again.

Fetch and carry

Many dogs love fetching games, although they may be reluctant to return the spoils to their owners. With a little perseverance, you can train even the worst hoarder to become a great collector. At the same time, you'll double your dog's exercise and improve your own flexibility and coordination!

No game is fun if it becomes forced, so listen to your dog and allow him to dictate the proceedings to a certain extent. Some breeds, such as Labradors and Golden Retrievers, are natural fetchers, whereas others aren't so keen. Continue only as long as your dog is having fun, then move on to something else. He'll soon get the idea.

Step-by-step fetch

Fetching and retrieving stimulates your dog and allows him to use most of his senses, as well as his muscles!

Left Reaching for or leaping up to catch a ball or toy is a great stretching exercise for dogs.

Above Although not all dogs are natural fetchers, most will enjoy collecting a favorite toy or ball to bring back to you.

1 Most dogs are happy to run after a toy or ball that's been thrown. When he begins the chase, shout "Fetch!" and offer praise when he retrieves the object.

2 When your dog collects his bounty, say "Come." When he begins his return, offer encouragement and praise.

3 If your dog loses interest and wanders off, begin again from the initial throwing point until he gets the idea.

4 When your dog (eventually) returns to you, say "Sit." If he doesn't automatically drop the toy or ball, offer a treat as a trade.

5 When he does drop the ball, make sure you praise him to high heaven.

Left Choose balls that are appropriate for your dog's size—small enough for him to get a good grasp, but not so small that he'll choke.

Left Don't let your dog get too attached to one specific toy or ball because he may refuse to hand it over.

Left Offer your dog a different toy to encourage him to drop the one he has just retrieved.

Curb the obsession

Some dogs become devoted to the same toy and refuse to hand it over. It is possible to prevent this behavior by using a few different toys, and by swapping a new toy when the old one is retrieved. This is also a useful training tip, because it teaches dogs to return items when requested, in the full knowledge that they will get something better.

Drop!

Teach your dog the "Drop!" command, especially if he's reluctant to part with his toys. Hold your hand gently under his jaw when he has a toy in his mouth, and say "Drop!" Carefully retrieve the ball from his mouth and praise him. Then return the ball so that your dog knows he won't be deprived of his toy because he has obeyed you.

Game time

Playing games is one of the best ways to both stimulate your dog's mind and provide vigorous exercise. In addition, it enables you to establish your leadership in an enjoyable way. Games of fetch with balls, Frisbees, or squeaky toys are excellent ways to give your dog a good workout without getting too sweaty yourself.

The sporting breeds, such as Retrievers and Spaniels, are naturals at playing fetch and easily give up objects. Other breeds, such as Terriers, are more likely to hold on to toys or balls no matter what.

All dogs can be taught to drop an object on command (*see opposite*). However, don't pick anything edible, such as rawhide, for your dog to retrieve—you'll never get it back!

And what about you?

There's no doubt that you can sit down and throw, using the minimum of effort; however, you can also turn a game of fetch into something more energetic:

● Stretch your arms out as far as possible when throwing, to maximize your flexibility.

● Aim for a particular spot to improve your coordination.

● Bend and reach when throwing or collecting the returns—every muscle that you push to its limits will respond by becoming more pliant.

● Take a running jump when you throw, to raise your heart rate and provide a short burst of oxygenated blood to your system.

● Chase after the toy with your dog, and play a game of tug-of-war from time to time, to keep up the variety. Make it clear, however, that when you say "Drop," the game is over.

Above Frisbees are great doggie toys, but make sure they aren't made of flimsy plastic, which could splinter.

Let's play ball!

Not all dogs are natural soccer stars, or willing to play left field or catcher, but ball games are great for overall exercise and help to keep *you* fit as well. Because they are fun, they'll keep your dog motivated for hours on end. When your dog runs, jumps, or sprints after a ball, he's not only getting fit, but is training his motor sequences, reactions, and spatial visualization. It's important, however, to get the ball size right, and to make sure it is sturdy enough to resist the overexcited clamping of jaws.

Below Dogs love to learn new games and soccer is good exercise for dogs of all ages.

Which ball?

For rolling and throwing, small balls made of hard rubber are a good choice. They shouldn't be small enough to cause choking, but they should be durable and enable your dog to get a good hold on them. Leather or heavy plastic soccer balls are ideal for some games. Although tennis balls are fine in the short term, the fiber covering will eventually damage your dog's teeth. Choose light balls—from hand size to no

Caution!

Take care not to leave lightweight, air-filled balls with your dog, as he might bite them and swallow the pieces when they burst.

more than soccer-ball size. Your dog should be trained to relinquish the ball upon the command "Drop!" (*see page 76*).

Which game?

Try some of the following ball games to add variety to the usual fetch and carry. Your dog will love them!

Monkey-in-the-middle

Gather with some friends or family members in a circular formation, with your dog in the middle. Throw a small ball at dog height between yourselves and encourage your dog to try to catch it. When he succeeds, allow him to stop and play for a while before starting again.

Ball-boxing

This is one occasion when it's okay to throw a ball directly at your dog, but only if the ball is lightweight and air-filled. Encourage your dog to jump into the air at the right moment and propel the ball back to you (or in your direction) using his muzzle. Choose a nice grassy area, because frequent falls are a likely consequence of this exciting game.

Doggie ball

Once you've mastered ball-boxing, you can move on to net games! Teach your dog the "Push" command:

1 Place a treat under a ball. Your dog will push the ball forward to get the treat.

2 Say "Push" at the same time that he attempts this maneuver.

3 Repeat a couple of times, and then start to reward your dog every other time, until the treats are no longer required.

Right Dogs make excellent dribblers. Reward him when he masters nose-pushing and then move on to cones.

Left Why not try doggie volleyball? Any size of soft ball will do.

Next, get your dog to stand behind a low net, no higher than his neck to begin with. Gently throw a soft ball just above his head and say "Push." It will take some time for him to come to grips with the idea of pushing something airborne, but he'll soon figure it out. Many dogs will instantly try to catch the ball, but be firm and continue to ask your dog to push it. It doesn't matter if he gets it back over the net. Praise him every time he manages to make contact with his muzzle or head and the ball.

When he's learned to bounce the ball on his nose, head, or muzzle, you can encourage him to aim it back over the net. Volleyball!

Soccer star

Play soccer with your dog as you would with any opponent—try to dribble around him, get the ball past him toward a goal, lift it over him, and encourage him to push the ball with his muzzle and feet. It doesn't take long for most dogs to catch on to the game, although they will be unlikely to score a goal! Make it fun—shout and praise him when he gets the ball away from you, and encourage him to allow you to get it away from him, too, as part of the game.

You will sometimes need to slow the pace during these exciting games and give your dog commands such as "Sit" or "Down." This way he will always know that you are in control.

Cone slalom

Set up a series of cones and teach your dog to dribble around them with a "Weave" command. Begin by encouraging him to push the ball upon command and start the game with his left shoulder nearest to the first obstacle in a short course of cones.

1 Tell your dog to "Push," and as he approaches a cone, to "Weave." Drop a few treats in the pattern that you hope he'll follow through the obstacle course.

2 Lead him around the obstacles, saying "Weave" as you do so.

3 You'll undoubtedly have to lead your dog around the obstacles a number of times before he can do it on his own. Praise him highly and offer a treat every time he reaches the end of the course.

Above Teaching your dog to dribble around cones helps develop his coordination.

Caution!

Never throw a ball directly at a dog's face, and never play catch with small balls. Aggression and, in the latter case, choking, are real risks.

What about you?

All of these games can be adapted to push yourself as well. Stretch yourself up and into the air while throwing; jump and run when playing soccer or monkey-in-the-middle; and perfect a great return when sending back the volleyball. Dribble around the cones yourself to show your dog how it's done. Every step and every bit of effort adds up to calories burned and enhanced fitness.

Agility for you both

Agility courses do just what the name suggests: encourage agility and flexibility while improving fitness on all levels and providing essential stimulation for your dog. What's more, you can join in the fun and experience the same benefits yourself.

Caution!

Never set bars or jumps too high. You may think your dog will get a better workout by pushing himself, but it is more likely to result in injury.

Right Running and jumping provides aerobic exercise and increases your dog's flexibility.

Agility courses are, effectively, obstacle courses with elements such as balancing on logs or beams, which promotes dexterity and nimbleness. Most dogs enjoy racing around a circuit and are eager to please, so make sure you offer plenty of praise for everything your dog masters. Equally, however, if you have a reluctant pet on your hands, see if you can encourage him to try at least a few of the activities.

Setting up your own course

There are a number of elements that you will want to incorporate, including those that encourage balance, weaving, jumping, tunneling, and flat-out running through different objects, such as hoops. It needn't be expensive to set up a course; in fact, most items can be purchased second hand or adapted from children's toys.

Agility basics

Here are some basic tips for choosing agility equipment and setting up a course to ensure safety and avoid any injuries:

● Choose a place that provides a safe landing if your dog falls and also offers a non-slip surface. A lawn is ideal.

● Select materials that will not injure your dog—light plastic tubing, wood, and PVC bars and fittings are all good bets.

● Anything over which your dog is expected to jump, such as a bar or a hurdle, should be unfixed, but supported so that it dislodges on contact. This prevents injuries. The bases, however, should be stable and unlikely to tip over on contact.

● Make sure you've got enough space between obstacles. Jumps require some running space for takeoff and landing—about five strides in advance and four afterward.

● Your dog will need to know the basic commands (*see pages 76–81*) before being taught to negotiate an agility course. During training, reward your dog with toys or a healthy snack when he completes a task successfully.

● Make sure you don't push your dog too hard, or force him to do something that he is afraid or reluctant to try. Be patient and work on one activity at a time.

Jumping

This activity is the core of most agility trials, and encourages your dog to use a number of muscle groups, which improves strength, coordination, and flexibility. You can purchase professional jumps or build your own. Set the height according to the size of your dog—no jump should be higher than shoulder height.

Above Start with low bars and offer plenty of praise when your dog goes over on command.

Jumps can consist of a light plastic tube set across two cones, a "window" hung in a square frame through which your dog jumps, an old tire fixed in roughly the same manner, or something handheld, such as a hula hoop. Some jumps can be more strenuous: for example, you can place two bars a few inches apart to produce a more difficult jump.

Jump training

Not all dogs are natural jumpers, so take it slowly and begin with low heights, gradually working up to shoulder height.

1 Attach your dog's leash and jog him up to and over the jump.

2 Say "Over" as you do so. Use this command every time he jumps.

3 Give plenty of praise when he gets it right. Offer a toy as a reward after several jumps.

4 Continue to jump (by yourself if necessary) until he masters the game.

5 Stop at the jump and encourage him to do it himself.

6 Gradually stop further away from the jump each time, saying "Over."

7 You will eventually be able to point and give the command to get results.

Right You can include two or more hurdles, as long as your dog can easily master the distance between them, and the jumps are not too high for him.

Moving on to hurdles

Hurdles are effectively a series of jumps over which your dog will leap. Begin with one hurdle and gradually add others until you have three or four in a row. Make sure you set them up in a straight line with at least five paces between them; hurdles on angles can cause your dog to strain muscles and ligaments as he tries to negotiate a new position.

1 When your dog can leap over one hurdle easily, add another.

2 Jog beside him to the second jump and give the command "Over!"

3 Jump over the second hurdle together. Then start at the beginning and jump over both the hurdles together.

4 When your dog is confident, allow him to do it on his own, using a hand signal while you say "Over," and then gradually using just the signal to indicate that he should jump.

Walking in circles

In professional agility setups, dogs are expected to be able to walk backward and in circles. These activities stimulate your dog and encourage good coordination.

1 Stand in front of your dog with a treat held in a closed hand.

2 Don't give up the treat. When your dog realizes that he can't have it, he will start to back away.

3 As he steps back, say "Back," and then offer the treat and plenty of praise.

4 Try this a number of times until your dog walks backward of his own accord; over time, increase the distance.

Above Always offer a reward when your dog gets it right the first few times.

Now that your dog has mastered this, you are ready to move on to walking in circles:

1 Place an obstacle alongside your dog—a cone, a bucket, or a chair is a good choice.

2 Lure him around the obstacle with a treat in your hand, while saying "Around."

3 Give him the treat when he has done a full circle around the obstacle.

4 Continue until he will circle the obstacle upon command.

5 Now repeat the procedure, getting your dog to walk backward!

Above When your dog has mastered walking in circles, he will be capable of negotiating obstacles.

Hula hoops

This is an easy agility activity and can be undertaken anywhere—as long as there is a nonslip surface. Make sure you don't hold the hoop too high. No dog should ever jump higher than its shoulder.

1 Hold the hoop as steady as you can, at a low height. This will make the task less daunting for your dog.

2 Using your other hand, offer your dog a treat and say "Through."

3 Repeat, moving the hoop upward by 1 in (2.5 cm) each time. Continue to say "Through."

4 When your dog has mastered the basics, throw a treat through the hoop and say "Through." He will probably jump through the hoop without hesitation, but continue until he feels confident.

5 Gradually raise the hoop to shoulder height and continue the process.

6 When your dog can jump effortlessly through the hoop, he can graduate to a tire or a "window," which is normally fixed inside a frame.

Above Move the hoop up a little each time before your dog jumps through.

Weaving

Using your dog's new skills, and those he has developed for soccer dribbling (*see page 81*), set up a series of cones and encourage him to weave in and around them—walking forward and backward. You can use a ball or teach him to do it without.

(*see page 81*)

Caution!

Always sand and paint handmade equipment to prevent splintering. Alternatively, you can carefully glue down patches or strips of rubber to allow your dog to get a better grip.

Seesaw

This activity is great for your dog's balance, and the equipment can easily be manufactured using a wooden plank set over a solid base, which acts as a fulcrum. Choose lightweight lumber and use a nontoxic paint to smooth the surface and prevent splintering. Your dog will walk along the seesaw to the center (balance point), causing the other end to go down. He will then jump off the lowered end.

1 Encourage your dog with a treat to walk to the midpoint of the seesaw. Offer the treat as a reward when the seesaw begins to lower.

2 Lead him off the end of the seesaw, ensuring that he walks to the end of the plank and doesn't jump off it earlier.

3 Repeat the process several times, gradually withdrawing the reward.

Left Teaching your dog to walk along a seesaw is a great activity for improving his balance.

Above Your dog should be trained not to leave the pause table until he is given the command.

Pause for thought

A "pause take" is a 36 in (91 cm) square sturdy table or box, onto which your dog jumps and then sits or lies down. He should not jump off the table until given instructions by you. Your table should be sturdy, with a nonstick surface, and should be an easy height (no higher than shoulder height) for your dog to jump onto. This is a good calming exercise for excitable dogs, and encourages obedience and concentration.

1 Place a treat in the middle of the table to lure him up, and say "Table."

2 Command your dog to "Stay" or "Sit" when he reaches the top.

3 Wait a few seconds, making sure he sits calmly, and then say "Down."

4 If he jumps off the table early, start again, making it clear that he cannot jump down until given the cue.

5 Continue practicing until your dog can wait at least ten seconds before getting down.

Tunnels

Some dogs are frightened by the prospect of tunneling, but tunnels do form an exciting and essential part of most agility courses, encouraging dogs to crouch down and crawl, which is great for flexibility and muscle strength.

A child's tunnel with light wire casings and a rigid material that won't collapse (or be easily clawed through or chewed) is ideal. Most tunnels are between 12 and 15 ft (3.6–4.5 m) in length on a professional course, but the length isn't as important as the activity itself for novices. Always anchor your tunnel so that it can't move from side to side, and curl it slightly so that your dog can't see the other end.

1 Begin with a straight tunnel, so that your dog is not overawed by entering a dark space.

2 A short tunnel is best to begin with—many tunnels are accordion-style so that you can adjust their length.

3 Ask your dog to sit at one end of the tunnel. Kneel at the other end so he can see you.

4 Encourage him to go through, saying "Tunnel." Give him a treat when he exits.

5 When he's confident with a short tunnel, gradually increase the length, a little at a time. Continue to say "Tunnel" as he negotiates it.

Some tunnels are large for full-speed running; others are low and narrow to encourage crawling. Your dog will soon learn what to do in each. Continue to say "Tunnel" as he goes through.

6 Encourage your dog to run through the tunnel by running toward it yourself saying "Tunnel." Continue to run alongside it repeating "Tunnel" as he canters through.

7 Gradually curve the end of the tunnel so that he can't see it, and continue practicing until he's mastered going through it.

Above Some dogs are wary of entering tunnels at the outset. Kneel down at the other end so he can see you.

Left Start with a short tunnel and gradually make it longer as your dog becomes more confident.

Time trials

When you and your dog are approaching optimum fitness, you can move on to timing yourself around a circuit. Set up the various obstacles in a circular pattern, with plenty of room between them. Add as few or as many as your dog will enjoy and manage comfortably. Always warm up before you begin (*see page 58*). This is a great way to improve your fitness and that of your dog, and the competitive element is not only motivating, but adds to the fun.

Above Keep your dog on a short leash when you first teach him to go around the agility course.

Right Run alongside your dog at the outset so he understands what is expected of him.

Far right Stand on the other side of hoops and tunnels and encourage him to go through.

1 Go around the course together, walking quickly and making sure your dog can manage everything himself.

2 Take the speed up to a trot and go around the course again.

3 Finally, set off on the course together at the word "Go," doing all the jumps yourself and even crawling through the tunnels. Your dog will soon understand what is required, and will realize that he shouldn't skip stages.

4 Keep sessions short at the outset, to prevent him from becoming bored.

5 After some practice sessions, he can do it alone. You may need to run ahead first, encouraging him to follow, but eventually he'll get the idea and perform the whole circuit at the word "Go."

6 Time yourselves and work to improve your times by a few seconds each week.

7 If you are in an energetic mood, do the course yourself—or whenever you need a good workout!

Workouts on wheels

Many dogs are naturals when it comes to accompanying you on your wheels, but it's important that you take precautions to prevent injury or overexertion. What's more, some breeds are simply not designed to keep up with a steady, quick pace (*see page 69*).

Above Make sure your dog is happy to stay close on a special leash before you begin cycling with him.

Cycling

Cycling is excellent, effective exercise for you, burning some 800 calories an hour; for an athletic and very fit dog, running alongside can provide a great workout that it might be difficult for you to provide otherwise. Some sled dogs are conditioned for winter by being run alongside a cyclist. Always start your program slowly, building up both distance and speed over time. Don't even consider it if your dog is not energetic and extremely fit, and always check with your vet first.

Getting started

When you first start, walk your bicycle slowly, talking to your dog the whole time. Praise him when he stays by your side and doesn't yank on the leash or stop unexpectedly. Once your dog has demonstrated that he can keep pace next to you, get on your bicycle and pedal a short distance. Increase the distance slowly as you build up your dog's endurance, confidence, and ability to keep pace with you.

Left When you start out, walk your bicycle and praise your dog when he walks to heel.

Cycling considerations

There are a number of bicycle attachments specially designed to keep your dog beside you, and to prevent him from upsetting your balance. Never tie a leash to your handlebars! Some dogs can be trusted to jog alongside your bicycle, in which case you may not need a leash—particularly if you are in a quiet open space.

Bring along plenty of water, and stop when your dog shows signs of being tired. Some dogs are happy to sit and have a drink while you literally ride circles around them!

Cycling provides a good workout if your time is tight—you can achieve the same benefits in about half the time it takes to jog or walk briskly. Cycling is also low-impact, so if you suffer from joint problems, it provides great aerobic exercise without the same potential for injury or pain.

Don't cycle with...

Your dog will be required to jog or run at a fairly quick pace alongside a bicycle or skater, and some breeds are simply not designed for this. Avoid cycling, skating, and jogging with these dogs:

- Boston Terriers
- Boxers
- Brussels Griffons
- Cavalier King Charles Spaniels
- Chinese Shar-peis
- English and French Bulldogs
- Japanese Chins
- Lhasa Apsos
- Pekingese
- Pugs
- Shih Tzus
- Staffordshire Bull Terriers

How long?

Thirty minutes is a good workout for most dogs and their owners, but you may need to start with ten-minute cycling sessions and work up to this gradually. Alternatively, choose to walk alongside your bike for ten minutes, cycle for ten, and then walk for ten, until both you and your dog feel ready to stop. Highly energetic dogs can work up to sixty-minute rides, with plenty of breaks.

Inline skating

Inline skating is fantastic exercise for you. Not only is it fun, it is an easy way to trim away the pounds and improve your circulation, heart, and lungs. Your leg muscles will also get a full workout! What's more, a fit dog can accompany you and achieve the same benefits.

Inline skating, like cycling, is low-impact, which makes it a good alternative to running or jogging for anyone with problematic knees or tendons. Fewer people suffer injuries from inline skating than from jogging or running, and studies show that skating raises your heart rate even higher than jogging does.

One Wisconsin study found calorie-burning rates in moderately fit individuals during inline skating to be as high as 19 calories per minute, enough to trim away up to 5 oz (150 g) of fat in sixty-one minutes. You would have to run about 10 miles (16 km) in the same timeframe to burn as many calories.

Above Before attempting to skate with your dog, make sure you practice on your own until you get the hang of it.

Caution!

Inline skating is only low-impact if you don't fall, so make sure you stay on your feet and wear appropriate protective equipment. Avoid it if you have bone or joint problems.

Inline skating with your dog

Many experts recommend that you not inline skate with your canine friend because dogs can easily catch you off balance, causing injuries, some of which may be serious.

Make sure you get the hang of skating before involving your dog. Inline skating can be mastered in a few sessions, but falling with a leash in your hand can cause injuries to you and your dog, and ruin the whole experience. Be sure to wear the recommended protective equipment, and don't go any faster than a pace at which you know you can stop.

Keep your leash short. Long leashes will allow your dog to cross in front of you and you'll end up running him over. A length of 6 ft (1.8 m) is a good start. And always use a gentle leader or Halti collar, so that you aren't pulled or pulling. Keep an eye on your dog. If he's struggling to keep up, stop, or skate around him while he takes a break.

Work up slowly to longer distances. Start with ½ mile (0.8 km) and increase the momentum until you are both ready to stop.

Right Keep your dog on a short leash to keep him by your side so he doesn't pull you off balance.

Safety issues

Take precautions to ensure maximum safety when skating with your dog:
- Avoid areas with traffic, other skaters, children, and bumpy surfaces (which may cause you and your dog to go sprawling).
- Skate in the early morning or late evening when it's less busy and cooler for you both.
- Try to find a path beside a grassy parkway, so your dog can run on the grass, which is better for his joints and paws.
- Watch your speed.

Water workouts

Most dogs love water and the opportunity to cool down and play in a new environment. Water sports, such as swimming, will also provide you with an opportunity to achieve effective, low-impact exercise and give your muscles a good workout too.

Swimming increases flexibility and stamina, and is excellent for people with joint problems. It's a gentle way for those who are overweight to begin being more active.

Swimming also uses more of the overall muscle mass of the body than almost any other form of exercise, and gives you an upper- and lower-body workout, unlike running or cycling. Specifically, swimming and other forms of water exercise, such as water aerobics, offer remarkable cardiovascular benefits.

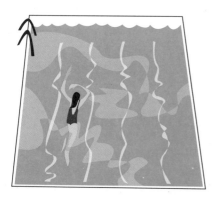

How much?

To get the best benefits from swimming you need to work on endurance, which builds up muscle and improves cardiovascular fitness. Nonstop lap-swimming for thirty minutes will build endurance. Stop when you are tired, and gradually add an extra five minutes to your routine until you can master sixty minutes with only a few breathing breaks. If you are playing or doing other water activities with your dog, use the same calculation. As long as you are constantly active, you'll be burning calories and working your heart and muscles.

Involving your dog

Swimming is great exercise for dogs, particularly those with joint or bone problems, and those that are aging. The water will support your dog's body and enable him to play and become fit with a minimum of stress on creaking joints.

If you live near lakes or ponds (rivers are not ideal because of the strong currents that can flow under the surface), swimming can be a source of

free entertainment and exercise and, if you live in the right climate, a year-round activity. Always be sure, however, that swimming for dogs is legal and that the water is free from pesticides. Believe it or not, there are indoor and outdoor facilities available in some countries just for pets to swim in.

Can my dog swim?

Some breeds of dog are not natural swimmers and these include:

- Bulldogs
- Basset Hounds
- Dachshunds
- Greyhounds and other low-fat breeds, which can suffer from hypothermia. However, that's not to say they can't enjoy the water! Even nonswimmers are happy to play in the shallows and catch a ball or Frisbee, or to venture into slightly deeper waters to find a favorite toy.

Experts claim it's a myth that some dogs cannot swim; although the bodies of certain breeds are not designed for swimming, if they become accustomed to water at an early age, are "taught" to swim, and have the assistance of a life preserver, they can most certainly join you in the water.

Right Not all dogs love water. Never force a dog to swim and keep a close eye on him if he does go in.

Caution!

Never, ever throw your dog into the water. This will only increase his anxiety and will probably turn him off the idea of swimming altogether.

Left Take the plunge with your dog until he gets used to entering the water.

Make it fun

Start by playing in the water, throwing toys to fetch, and jumping in and out. Encourage your dog to swim alongside you when you swim laps and to try to catch you. Encourage him with praise and egg him on by holding a toy in your fastest swimming hand.

In the beginning

To introduce your dog to the water for the first time, be prepared to get wet! Enter the water and coax your dog in by calling to him in an upbeat way. You can use treats or throw floating toys to encourage him to enter. Also, "monkey see, monkey do" works well in this situation: Having another dog happily swimming around will definitely encourage your pup to take the plunge. If your dog is hesitant, take a break and try again later.

Games

You can also play different games in the water. Swim to the other side of the pool or pond and hold up a toy; as he moves toward it, change the direction of the throw and try to get there before him.

If your dog is a natural soccer player, invest in some floatable obstacles and encourage him to nose a ball around them. Do the same yourself with another ball, and keep up the pace.

Safety measures

Here is some advice to take into account to make swimming with your pooch as safe and problem-free as possible:

- Avoid areas with boats, water skiers, or young children, who may frighten your dog or cause him to become overexcited.
- Thoroughly rinse away saltwater or chlorine from your dog after swimming.

It can be difficult to give an overweight dog sufficient exercise on land without overstressing joints and bones. Swimming provides excellent complementary supported exercise.

- Make sure there is a bank or shore to get in to and out of the water safely.
- Give your dog time after his swim to run around and dry off. This will help prevent chills and sore limbs.
- Offer fresh water to drink if you are swimming in a pond or the ocean, both of which are inappropriate for dogs to drink from.
- If you have a pool, raise any ladders and lock the pool gates to prevent unsupervised swimming. Many people have lost dogs in tragic drowning accidents in backyard pools because the dogs couldn't get out and no one was there to save them.

Life preservers

If you're planning to make swimming a regular part of your dog's exercise routine, a canine life preserver may be a very valuable purchase. This can help keep your dog afloat if he's accidentally knocked into the water or if he becomes tired quickly.

Left Your dog may just enjoy a good splash, which is still a form of exercise. Don't push him to do more.

Cooling down

When you are all fired up after exercise, cooling down may seem unimportant, but studies show that it has a multitude of benefits and can help both you and your dog move toward peak fitness with greater ease.

Your cool-down should consist of a gentle five-minute light jog or walk, followed by five to ten minutes of stretching. What does this do? Cooling down:

- Lowers your body temperature
- Helps rid your body of waste products, which can cause pain and cramping
- Relaxes the muscles and increases their range of motion

- Helps to prevent dizziness or fainting
- Signals your body to stop secreting adrenaline, which can cause problems with blood-sugar levels and raise your blood pressure
- Allows your heart to return to its resting rate.

Which stretches?

The warm-up exercises on pages 58–59 are all appropriate for cooling down, too. Add the following to get a good whole-body stretch and cool-down:

Chest stretch

1 Stand up straight, with your feet slightly wider than shoulder-width apart, and your knees slightly bent.

2 Hold your arms out to the side, parallel with the ground and your palms facing forward.

3 Stretch your arms behind you, as far back as possible. You should feel a good stretch across your chest.

Upper back stretch

1 Stand tall, feet slightly wider than shoulder-width apart, knees slightly bent.

2 Interlock your fingers and push your hands as far away as possible from your chest, allowing your upper back to relax.

3 You should feel the stretch between your shoulder blades.

Shoulder stretch

1 Stand tall, feet slightly wider than shoulder-width apart, knees slightly bent.

2 Place your right arm parallel with the ground across the front of your chest.

3 Bend the left arm up and use the left forearm to ease the right arm closer to your chest. You will feel the stretch in your right shoulder.

4 Repeat the stretch with the other arm. Then begin again. Two or three good shoulder stretches is about right.

Canine cooling

A slow, gentle walk with plenty of "sniffs" on the way home is ideal to cool down your dog. You'll notice that he will naturally stretch himself as he moves, and stop to rest or reduce his activity after a long session.

Most dogs love a little massage, which can help to reduce muscle tension and prevent the build-up of waste products in the muscles. Pull his legs gently as you massage—a few minutes is plenty—and as you bend over, you'll be stretching yourself too. Always offer your dog a cold drink—or if it is very hot, a splash in the local water hole or sprinkler, to bring his body temperature down to safe levels.

Maintaining the program

For maximum success, you need to treat your health and fitness goals as a priority. Once you are both on your way to achieving your ultimate weight and ideal fitness levels, you can change the rules a little to suit your lifestyle.

Keeping on the go

Continuing to increase your exercise levels on a weekly basis will keep up the momentum. If you are bored by the regular routine, try some of the other options outlined in this book. Exercise is not all about walking or running; you can play with your dog and increase your heart rate simply through regular games. Also consider the options that don't involve your dog. You may want to learn to ski, rock climb, or gorge walk, try Pilates or yoga, or simply join human friends on the tennis court. Use your improved fitness to explore the opportunities and make the most of what you can achieve.

Left Once you are both on track to achieving your goals, you can tailor your program to your newfound health and fitness levels.

If you are worried that your canine friend is missing out, splurge on the occasional play session with a willing teenager, who can run him ragged while you look after your own needs.

The 20:80 rule

If you've been diligent with your nutrition plan, you can now take a little step back. The secret to maintaining your weight is to carry on with your regular exercise routine, and to stick to a healthy eating program—most of the time. Once you've reached your target weight you can start to indulge yourself a little more. As long as 80 percent of your meals (and calories) are based on the pyramid structure (see page 37), you can introduce a few treats: 20 percent, that is. From now on, 20 percent of your diet can be fun—that extra glass of wine, a slice of chocolate cake, or a creamy treat at your local pasta bar. If you have treats occasionally, you are less likely to stray from your overall goal.

Don't lower your goals

As long as you continue with the same level of activity, or increase it slightly, you'll be on target for maintenance. Achieving goals doesn't mean stopping dead once you feel fit; it means continuing—for life. Your dog, too, will by now understand his new routine and eagerly await his exercise sessions with you. He'll also be accustomed to his new diet, and his mood and overall behavior will be much improved.

Staying motivated

If you've reached a good level of fitness, or find you have hit a plateau and are finding it hard to keep yourself motivated, it's worth investing a little more energy in fine-tuning your program to suit you and your interests.

1 It's important to continue to set goals— if you aren't aiming toward something, you are unlikely to stick to a routine. Writing your goals down can also help you stay motivated.

2 Don't forget to reward yourself when you reach those goals (or are even halfway there)—a dinner out, a weekend away, a new article of clothing, anything goes. If you've got something to look forward to, you are more likely to continue.

3 Remember to be flexible. If you're too busy to work out, or simply don't feel up to it, take a day or two off. The important thing is to get back on track again when you feel better.

Introducing variety

Even the best exercise programs can become routine and a little boring over time; by incorporating a bit of variety and different types of exercise, you can ensure that both you and your dog are motivated to continue.

Change the pace

Make some of your walks or runs faster and others slower. Choose your pace according to your mood and the weather, and slow it down to enjoy the sights, or pick it up to reach your target heart rate. Make the most of interval training, in which you run, walk, and jog for ten minutes at a time, and then alternate exercises.

Alter your route

Choose different parks or woodlands for your daily walk; find new streets or back roads to investigate; go a little further away on the weekends to visit the beach or a lake, or to negotiate some steeper inclines. Changing your lifestyle to one that is more active involves seeking out new options and taking advantage of them.

Team up with some friends

Both dogs and their owners like a little companionship, so why not meet up with like-minded friends to explore the countryside on the weekend, walk in the woods, race in the park, or skate along the river? Join a group of dog owners who are eager to explore the options. Your dog will be stimulated and so will you, and regular commitments such as this will encourage you to continue.

Left Explore different territory and try new activities to add variety to your routine.

Above If your dog has been bred to pull, he could learn to sleigh during the winter months.

Seasonal fun

A walk in the middle of winter can be a dire prospect, particularly if the snow reaches above your knees. There may also be times during the summer when vigorous exercise is too dangerous in the heat. Be inventive. Look up local organizations that host indoor activities for dogs and their owners. Set up an obstacle course in your own home. Learn how to cross-country ski or swim, and take your pet along. The options are limitless, as long as you look for them. Did you know, for example, that there are a number of organizations catering for dogs of almost *all* breeds to learn to sleigh? Why not join in?

Up the ante

Add some variety to your daily routine. A few push-ups, sit-ups, deep squats, a session with free weights, or a class at the gym will increase your resistance (strength) exercises, building muscle, which in turn increases your body's fat-burning potential.

Set some new goals

Once you've achieved your goal, you may need to reach for greater heights. Give yourself regular challenges—teach your dog to swim, for example, or master inline skating. In the kitchen, you can teach yourself some new recipes, and master different cuisines—Thai and Japanese cooking, for example, are very nutritious and often low in calories. Make your meals fun and you'll enjoy your maintenance program even more.

Older dogs

It's not always easy or safe to encourage older dogs to keep up with your new regime, but exercise is essential, whatever your dog's age, to keep him fit and to prevent many of the illnesses associated with old age.

Your older dog

As dogs age, they may experience loss of mental agility. Exercise can help to slow down this process, by increasing the amount of oxygenated blood to the brain. Quite apart from anything else, exercise helps to ward off many of the conditions associated with aging, such as osteoporosis, arthritis, heart disease, diabetes, and overweight.

Wear and tear

As a dog gets older, you'll notice a decrease in his energy levels. He becomes tired more easily and likes to nap often. He may experience stiffness in his leg, hip, and shoulder joints. This could just be normal wear and

Above Older dogs still need exercise. Just decrease the duration and slow down the pace.

tear, or it could be the result of an old injury or a sign of arthritis. While some exercises such as running might be out of the question, there's no reason why your dog can't try some gentle swimming (low-impact), jog slowly beside you, or take long, regular walks on even terrain.

How geriatric is your dog?

Generally, larger dogs begin aging earlier than smaller breeds. For example, if your dog is a St. Bernard, he could be considered a geriatric dog as early as six years old. But medium-sized dogs don't usually show signs of aging until nine to eleven years. And small breeds like Toy Poodles probably won't show signs until they're at least eleven. See page 49 for more information on the aging categories for different breeds.

Above You may be able to go further and faster than your older dog, but you don't need to leave him at home. He can rest under a tree while you work out.

Exercising with older dogs

If you play fetch with your older dog, throw the ball or toy a little closer than you did when he was younger, and repeat the toss fewer times. After a point, it is probably advisable to stop playing fetch and to concentrate on walking or swimming.

Keep in mind that your dog will do anything to please you. This means he may tend to become overexerted in running or playing, simply because he thinks that's what you expect. You will need to judge the situation carefully and to adjust the strenuousness and duration of the exercise accordingly.

At-home exercise is also a good alternative for older dogs. Use a carpeted area for the session, and one of your dog's favorite toys. You can play a modified game of fetch in a relatively small area. You might also want to play a game that involves your dog doing roll-overs or lying on his back to kick the air.

Two shorter walks will be less stressful on aging joints than one long walk. The walks can be quite brisk, provided your vet has given approval. Twenty minutes is enough for most older dogs.

Index

Acknowledgments

Ivy Press would like to thank everyone at Hearing Dogs for Deaf People (www.hearingdogs.org.uk) for their invaluable advice on the text. Thank you also to the owners and their dogs who did such a wonderful job at the photo shoot: Lisa Coles and Kia, Tom Green and Fizz, and Jenny Palser and Pippa.